W9-AQG-848

WITHDRAWN

QUESTAR PUBLISHERS, INC.

I NEED YOU

Being Friends with Your Grandkids

C.G. "SPIKE" & DARNELL WHITE

QUESTAR PUBLISHERS, INC.
Sisters, Oregon

I NEED YOU
© 1989 by C. G. "Spike" and Darnell White
Published by Questar Publishers, Inc.

Printed in the United States of America

ISBN 0-945564-23-6

Cover Design by Jerry Werner

Dedication

These memories and musings we dedicate to our grandchildren,
with special thanks for loving us and making our lives fulfilled.
(As we sometimes tease them, they're all
"pretty good kids, for grandkids!")

TO:

CODY — Strong, solid, studious, serious;
strives to play football;
"Mr. Stud"

LANCE — Loves life, everybody, and the Lord;
busy, involved, action-packed, awesome;
"Mr. Triathlete"

SCOTT — Loves "home," family ties, white-water
adventures; big smile, big heart, talented;
"Mr. Wholesome"

WESLEY — Most happy fellow; turned on
by people of all ages;
"Mr. Talk-Show Host"

JAMIE JO — Loves animals, her cousins, and
the outdoors; loyal, dependable, compassionate;
"Miss 'I'm Third' "

COURTNEY — Disciplined, organized,
exciting, energetic, electrifying;
"Miss Broadway"

BRADY — Sensitive, solid,
sweet, smart; deserves to be...
"Mr. Special"

COOPER — Congenial, content,
conscientious, devoted, delightful;
"Mr. Cool and Right"

BRANDI — "New kid on
our block"; delicious;
"Little Miss Warm and Winsome"

Contents

INTRODUCTION

T HE TITLE *I NEED YOU* tells it like it is:
Grandchildren need their grandparents.
And I need *you,* too.

After reading this book, you will know me
better than I know you. I wish it were not that
way. I would like to be there in person beside
you, listening to *you* tell me ways to be a better
grandmother, a better friend, a better mother
and mother-in-law. I could learn from you. I'm
sure you could help me!

I'm no one special as far as credentials go. I
don't have a Ph.D. in GP (grandparenting). I am
like Wilbur in *Charlotte's Web,* who, after Charlotte praised him, replied, "But I'm not terrific,
Charlotte. I'm just average for a pig."

In this book I am not trying to convey in any
way, "Shape up! Get with it! Do right!" My
desire is to pass on to you some encouragement, maybe some ideas, even things you
know well but haven't practiced or introduced

in your own relationships with the family. And as I do, it's rather like the way we parents used to admonish our children — our advice was directed to to ourselves as much as (maybe more than) to the offspring.

I want to thank Don Jacobson, our publisher, and Thomas Womack, our editor, for giving us the opportunity to put it all down on paper. And if I can practice and perform it as well as write it, and if you can believe and practice it as much as read it, then we both will have benefitted and will make a difference in the lives we live.

I close (not quit) with a renewed vigor to keep it up, do it better, be alert to new ways and new ideas...and ENJOY it!

Again, regarding the title, *I NEED YOU:* Isn't that what it's all about — *wanting* to be needed?

With our grandchildren, let's be like the sign at the railroad crossing: STOP, LOOK, LISTEN (and I would add LOVE). If together we do these things (you with your family, me with mine), we'll leave this world a better place.

✿ ✿ ✿

INTRODUCTION

S INCE YOU'RE READING THIS, it's safe to assume you either *may* buy this book, or have bought or borrowed it. In any case, you're entitled to be informed that if you knew me, you'd be as surprised as I was when Questar asked me to contribute to the project.

Darnell and I have three sons and have had five daughters-in-law (which seems to be about par for the course nowadays, like it or not). These families have nine children who are our grandkids. Families like ours are not world-class, but not bush-league either.

I suppose the main reason we seem qualified to write this book is that we have shared in the lives of thousands (yes, thousands!) of families in our lifetime of involvement in operating Kanakuk-Kanakomo Kamps and their Christian/athletic programs for youth.

The sole purpose of our lives and our camps

can best be summed up in the words of the late Stuart Symington, former United States Senator: "Five of my grandchildren have benefitted physically and spiritually from the character-building summer camp operated by the White family. Each is far more able to handle the many problems facing our youth in the turbulent world today. Their aims and ideals are a practical illustration of all that is best about our beloved country."

We hope and pray that what follows will give you some how-to ideas, a lot of encouragement, a bit of consolation, and a general appreciation of the great adventure of grandparenting in these wild, weird, wonderful times we are living in.

And remember: HAVE FUN!

Thanks for listening.

✽ ✽ ✽

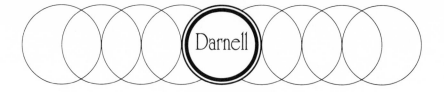

YOUR "PROGRAM"

Y OU MAY HAVE a hard time believing this, but I 've never been accused of saying, "Oh, I just happen to have a picture!"—and then whipping out a string of snapshots of our beautiful family members. A friend of mine who had no children once made the remark that she didn't relish having to look at wallet portfolios, so I made it a practice not to pull mine out to show strangers I meet and talk with. I really do *like* to see other folks' family photos...I just don't offer to show mine.

Now, if you come see us, you'll see *lots* of family pictures—taken at all ages—all around the house, and especially on the refrigerator and freezer doors. All over these cork-covered "iceboxes" are candid shots and cut-out faces, and our guests always pause there—they're fun to look at, even though the pictures are often the same as when our visitors were here the last time.

As you read this book (and if you ever come to see those pictures), it might be helpful to know who's who in our family, and the listing below will tell you.

It won't take long to learn the names—we're BIG only in togetherness and heart, but not in number.

THE CAST OF "CHARACTERS"

Number one son:	**Bob**
His wife:	**Mary Evelyn** (Mev)
Their sons:	**Lance** and **Scott**
Number two son:	**Bill**
His wife:	**Delisa**
Bill and Cyndi's sons:	**Cody** and **Wesley**
Delisa's daughter:	**Brandi**
Number three son:	**Joe**
His wife:	**Debbie Jo**
Their daughters:	**Jamie Jo** and **Courtney**
Their sons:	**Brady** and **Cooper**
Matriarch of the family:	**Pardner** (my 95-year-old mother)

See—that didn't take long, did it?

✿ ✿ ✿

I NEED YOU
Being Friends with Your Grandkids

KEEPING ON KEEPING ON

HE FIRST REQUIREMENT of grand-parenting is survival. **To become a "living legend" one must be living.**

To become a patriarch or a matriarch, "hanging in there" is paramount.

America's aerobics guru Dr. Ken Cooper made sweating stylish. After I've exercised, my wife says, "You smell tired"—I do, and I'm glad.

Older Americans especially, and many people worldwide, now have the know-how, the how-to, and the help not only to live to be grand-parents, but in many cases to become *old* grandparents, and even *great*-grandparents— and to feel good and be healthy doing it.

One of our full-time camp cooks in her sixties says, "Being a grandparent is grand, and being a great-grandparent is great!" She is both, so she knows.

Our youth camp construction crew has been together for more than twenty-five years. In that time we have built four girls' camps, four boys' camps, four wilderness camps, and four aquatic out-camps. These camps together include seven large swimming pools, twenty-two tennis courts, housing and dining facilities for 1,500 campers and counselors, six large gymnasiums, two play-domes, four boat docks, many acres of playing fields, six world-class water slides, two rope courses and rappelling towers...and on and on and on.

The construction crew that did all of the above is led by a carpenter-concrete man who is 78 years old.

The welder is 76 and he built all the pool equipment, trail rails, ski machines, slide towers, backstops, and weird contraptions for teaching and playing.

Our 76-year-old electrician has by himself established electrical service for what is the equivalent of several small towns.

The plumber is only in his late sixties, but his body has amassed a "million miles." He's plumbed all the pools, all the showers, and all the sewage treatment.

The painter, at 72, is a one-eyed genius who climbs, scrambles, mixes paint, and paints—and keeps all of us laughing and remembering the last laughs.

One of these oldsters, when asked how to get a job on our crew, replied, "Keep reading the obituaries, and when one of us dies, apply immediately."

★ ★ ★

All these oldsters are grandparents, and they squeeze in grandparenting along with their full-time construction jobs. In fact, two of them have each adopted and raised two grandchildren in their own homes. In both cases, they took in these kids because they didn't approve of the way they were being raised by their own parents. They have been successful with all four, who now are teenagers.

Billy Graham has said, "I have searched the Scriptures and found no record of any evangelist retiring." There is no mention in the Bible of any grandparent retiring either, and in fact, many biblical grandparents didn't really hit their stride until they attained their seventies and eighties.

We all need incentives for each effort and sacrifice we make. Longevity for the sake of longevity is not all that fulfilling, but we will be motivated by realizing that, as we lengthen our days, we are able to have an ever-growing part in so many other lives— namely, those of our children and their children, as well as others.

The real payoff to "keeping on keeping on" is in seeing how it all turns out—and, hopefully, being an aid and inspiration to each life we touch.

✶ ✶ ✶

MY CALLING

W HEN ANNOUNCEMENTS were made that our first grandchildren were on the way (yes, "grand*children*"—and not twins; our two daughters-in-law were "expecting" at the same time), I was typical, and became topical: *What will our grandchildren call me?*

I had friends with darling dubbings, and had heard of more: "G.G." (for Gorgeous Grandmother), "Honey," "Mimi," "Me-Mommy," and "Big Mama." (I've since heard such others as Ninee, Mums, Dee Dee, Bimp, Mama Too, Ninny, Mummy, Mawmaw, FaFa, Pee-Pie, Dado, and Mer.)

My Texas mother had her own unique solution: When grandchildren were born she knew right away she wanted them to call her "Pardner." To this day, though she's ninety-five-going-on-ninety-six, she is Pardner...and will not answer if her grandsons call her "Grandmother" or

"Granny"—which they will do sometimes just to tease her.

Having always admired Grandma Moses, not only for her warm and charming paintings but also for her renowned signature, I didn't spend much time on a new handle. Every child, I contended, deserves to have a "Gran'maw." *Gran'maw* to me truly describes the product: no additives, no preservatives, good for you, nutritional, Good Housekeeping Seal of Approval. The label tells it like it is. Besides, it was recognizable enough that our grandchildren would never have to explain who they're talking about when referring to me.

"Gran'maw" I became, just hoping the name gave off comfortable vibes.

Now Spike, their grandfather, wasn't that enamored with being "Gran'paw" or "Granddad." (Remember, in those days we were young and didn't look too bad —more like Ozzie and Harriet.) Instead he's been "Pappy" since the first grandchild called him "Happy" (it fits him well).

So that's who we are, Gran'maw and Pappy. The names have a nice ring, don't you agree? They just seem to go together, rather like "Ma and Pa Kettle."

A drawback to being called "Gran'maw" is that I don't like my husband calling me that—I'm not *his* grandmother! And it's a bit nettling when my own

✿ ✿ ✿

sons or "daughters-in-love" call me "Gran'maw." But I remember all the old advice: Let 'em think you don't care, and maybe they'll quit... Don't let 'em see you sweat... Play it cool... Sticks and stones may break my bones, but names will never hurt me.

Anyway, I'm used to it now, and being a good Gran'maw is my present mission on this earth. It's where I am—and I'm having the time of my life!

✿ ✿ ✿

ADAPTING

RECENTLY OUR DEAREST, longtime friends celebrated their golden wedding anniversary. The husband has had a successful career as an attorney, university professor, and judge. His wife is dedicated, imaginative, energetic, and happy as a wife, mother, and civic leader. Together they raised four beautiful, brilliant, talented daughters in a model, fun-filled home. Each of the daughters has married and had children, but their excellent background hasn't kept divorce from touching their lives. As the father sums it up: "I have four daughters, seven sons-in-law, and one more pending."

Darnell and I, who also recently celebrated our golden wedding anniversary, raised three sons. They too grew up in an action-packed, fun-loving, hard-working Christian family. Our sons also married—and we have had two "extra" daughters-in-law.

There just aren't a lot of "our kids" headed for their fiftieth wedding anniversaries... and consequently there are many grandkids who have more than two sets of grandparents.

Challenging? Yes. Sad? Certainly... but very interesting, nonetheless, as we sometimes "inherit" new and unexpected grandkids, and get to start all over loving them and keeping everyone happily involved in family events.

Confusing as all of it may be to kids and to grandparents, the good news is that **we grandparents *can* provide a stabilizing and inspiring presence to all concerned**—and as such are even more needed and more important than ever.

Our grandchildren are still our grandchildren, no matter where they live or with whom. When our "shuttle diplomacy" fails with the principals, then it must continue with the innocent victims who still have the same needs and problems, only more so. Kids can and do "roll with the punches," but as they do they more than ever need to be loved, looked after, assured, and included.

The hurt, disappointment, anger and confusion that are suffered during and following a divorce cannot be avoided, but they can be eased by daily phone calls, letters, visits, and by just being available and loving to "both sides" of the dilemma as well as to the innocent bystanders, our grandkids. It's so

✶ ✶ ✶

tough not to judge and take sides and give advice; but then, except for someone's spouse and children, who knows what it's *really* like to live with that person?

Picking up the pieces often takes years and the hurt can last a lifetime but the up side is that oftentimes grandparents emerge with greater and broader love and appreciation than ever.

We may look back and wonder, *Why didn't they ask us for help in the first place?* and *Why couldn't we see it coming and head it off?* But even if they had asked for our counsel, wouldn't they have done as we probably would have done, and gone their own way?

As parents and grandparents, all we can do, it seems, is to be available, inspirational, neutral, and adaptable. We raise our sons and daughters to adulthood and train them to cope—and apparently they must "do it their way," as Frank Sinatra sings.

Another singer, B. J. Thomas, asks, "Whatever happened to old-fashioned love... the kind that my Momma and Daddy had?" We know it still happens, but just not as frequently. Our job as "old-fashioned lovers" is to show that it *still works*—not only for husband and wife, but for our kids and grandkids, too, growing as their number may be.

As my spouse rationalizes, "The Lord gave me a big heart to keep on loving more new members of the

★ ★ ★

family." To me and to others, she shows the joy of giving love and receiving it—even in the midst of changes and challenges.

* * *

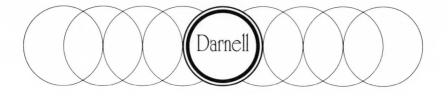

"I JUST DON'T HAVE TIME"

L AST SUMMER after camp season, Brady and Cooper, our two grandsons who live at Kanakuk Kamp in Branson, Missouri (where we also live), stayed for a few days and nights with Spike and me. The boys had bedrolls on the living-room floor.

One night Spike had gone to bed in the bedroom, and I was talking to the boys, telling them a story before hearing their prayers and saying good night.

Soon Cooper dropped off to sleep, leaving Brady and me to talk. Impulsively, I got out my dulcimer and played "My Grandfather's Clock" for him. He was fascinated by the instrument and the music.

Since the room was darkened—and I couldn't sing all the verses without looking at the words —I promised Brady, "Tomorrow night I'll get the words and sing it if you want me to."

Next night Brady remembered and reminded me. As I sang the sweet story in music form, I observed him wiping tears from his eyes.

After the song was sung, he sighed and said, "I just don't have much time...I stay so busy...I wish I had a clock like that."

 My Grandfather's Clock

My grandfather's clock was too large for the shelf
So it stood ninety years on the floor;
It was taller by half than the old man himself
Tho' it weighed not a penny weight more;
It was bought on the morn of the day he was born
And was always his treasure and pride;
And it stopped—short—never to run again
When the old man died.

(CHORUS:) Ninety years without slumbering —"tick-tock, tick-tock"—
His life seconds numbering —"tick-tock, tick-tock"—
And it stopped—short—never to run again
When the old man died.

In watching its pendulum swing to and fro
Many hours had he spent as a boy;
And in childhood and manhood the clock seemed to know
And to share both his grief and his joy;
For it struck twenty-four as he entered the door
With a blooming and beautiful bride;
And it stopped—short—never to run again
When the old man died.

 (CHORUS)

Brady really doesn't stay *that* busy, but he was in a sentimental mood at that moment, and it did seem to him that life was too rushed. However, I suspect that some children *are* too busy to adequately develop their own creative and exploratory talents. In many cases schedules are so programmed that the child seems to meet himself coming and going.

My grandfather said that of those he could hire
Not a servant so faithful he found;
For it wasted no time and had but one desire
At the close of each week to be wound;
And it kept in its place not a frown on its face
And its hands never hung by its side;
And it stopped—short—never to run again
When the old man died.

(CHORUS)

It rang an alarm in the dead of the night
An alarm that for years had been dumb;
And we knew that his spirit was plumbing for flight
That his hour of departure had come;
Still the clock kept the time with a soft muffled chime
As we silently stood by his side;
And it stopped—short—never to run again
When the old man died.

Ninety years without slumbering —"tick-tock, tick-tock"—
His life seconds numbering —"tick-tock, tick-tock"—
And it stopped—short—never to run again
When the old man died.

This reminds me of an amusing story recently told us by our son Joe, who is Brady and Cooper's father. He had been traveling for a few days showing "Kamp Movies" to people interested in our summer programs, and had just settled in at home only to discover the boys had been playing Nintendo on the television more than he thought beneficial to their development.

The next morning, Cooper was watching Joe shave. "Cooper," Joe announced to him, "I've already told Brady this: You and he are not to play Nintendo so much. I want you to get out and play and leave off the video games."

Cooper, who finds good in everything and never wants to make waves or hurt anyone, responded cheerfully, "Oh, that's all right, Dad; I really don't have time to play Nintendo. Joan comes in to tutor me all the time, so I'm really too busy...It's okay, Dad." (Of course Joan, his reading and speech tutor, works with Cooper only twice a week — one hour each lesson.)

There was no contest in either of the boys' reactions...they understood why Joe was denying them the time spent sitting and playing Nintendo. Children really like to be instructed and given house rules and guidelines that are solid and fair. It gives them stability and security, and when constructive criticism and admonitions come, they can accept them.

✿ ✿ ✿

We have observed that children of all ages, when raised to be independent and creative and to spend quiet times constructively, like themselves more and enjoy their own company. They're much happier and more contented. **In the push-and-pull world we live in, providing them with the opportunity to be quiescent is a special privilege grandparents can offer.**

In our house there are "just-for-kids" places for the grandchildren. Our front coat closet has made an ideal play area for the girls, with Barbie doll houses set up inside. Even after the girls have become older and less interested in playing "house," they often turn back time and become little girls again...closing the closet door and having quiet and uninterrupted enjoyment.

In the same closet is a toy box containing books for the kids to look at or bring to us to read with and to them. What a precious privilege to have a child sit close or in your lap and to share the magic words together!

There are simple PlaySkool toys, not sophisticated or complicated or space-dictated...the kind with which a child uses his own imagination and direction, making up the jargon while talking to the Weeble People and driving the little cars and trains. It's old-fashioned fun, peaceful and calming as a restful nap.

✿ ✿ ✿

We've also kept their fathers' and uncles' toys from the 1940s and 50s, and our grandchildren enjoy getting them out again and again.

We don't have an attic for the grandkids to explore, with its dusty, mysteriously inviting boxes. But there is a storage area under our downstairs steps that provides an avenue of adventure and imagination. Here we've put ladies' hats from long ago "Sunday-Morning-Go-to-Church" vintage, men's straw hats, bowlers, military caps, and weird and wonderful dresses and clothes — all of it perfect for playing "dress-up" or for dancing and performing in our "stage shows."

We've found that taking turns putting on plays and skits is great family fun and encourages naturalness and spontaneity for all. Everyone gets in the act, and everyone gets an Oscar! I sing or shuffle and share the limelight, too. I've never been able to carry a decent tune, but who cares? The kids don't!

Our oldest son, Bob, once presented us with a fine pool table that had been in a Mexican pool hall, the "Cinco de Mayo," about 75 or 100 years ago in Texas. That table has character — lots of scars and whittled-worn marks. If it could tell all its stories and we knew "Español," wouldn't that be a fiesta? Each of our grandchildren has learned to play pool on that table, holding a cue stick that's

✿ ✿ ✿

been sawed off to just the right size so it doesn't intimidate a potential hustler!

In the same room with the pool table there's a player piano, and when one or all gather to play pool or just watch the "shows," we sing together with gusto while the music rolls. We have some "oldies" you wouldn't believe! And when "Yes, Sir, That's My Baby" is played, it invariably brings out the straw hats and kazoos, and the Charleston dancers!

There are so many things to be done at Gran'maw and Pappy's house. And we want to keep it that way so grandkids will come back and come back and come back...and find some of the relaxing fun that all kids need.

✿ ✿ ✿

NEVER
TOO LATE

MY BEST FRIEND and sweetheart, the Gran'maw of so many, got "computerized" as a post-seventy activity. (One byproduct has been frequent word-processed, all-family letters.)

After outliving all my canoe partners, I took up kayaking at age seventy-two. It opened up a whole new whitewater world to me. I ran the Colorado River through the Grand Canyon, as well as the rest of "America's Ten Best Rivers" for kayaking. Now my grandkids are into the wild water, and loving it.

A ninety-eight-year-old friend's domino scorecard showed a record of 35 wins and only one loss.

Patriarch Caleb was still going and blowing and conquering at age eighty-five, and Israel was never the same again.

One of our camp's young coaches has a wall banner that reads, GO HARD OR GO HOME, and he preaches and teaches the same way. For older folks it could be paraphrased, GO HARD TILL YOU GO HOME.

Our camps have been blessed for twenty years with a camp nurse who has worked her grandkids' way through summer camp, season after season and grandkid after grandkid. She is seventy-two now, and still going strong.

Each issue of the AARP magazine *Modern Maturity* is filled cover-to-cover with real-life profiles of "born-again" oldsters in new careers, and jump-started second-time successes.

"It's later than we think"—that's true, but it's never *too* late, and the only place to start is where we are.

Grandchildren are frequently inspired when they see "last-ditch efforts," new bursts of speed, and just plain toughness in older loved ones.

So let's inspire them!

✳ ✳ ✳

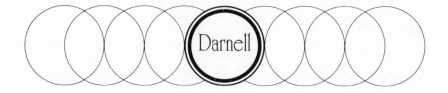

Darnell

MAKING MAGIC

T HERE'S A MAGIC that grandparents are endowed with—yet it's readily available only if we seek and use it. Even to grandparents with natural charisma—those whose qualities entice and invite children to reach out and share life with them—*working* at it is needed.

A good rule to work by is captured in the line Hoagy Carmichael wrote and sang: "You have to accentuate the positive and eliminate the negative."

Let's admit it: There are times (and more of them as we get older and slowed-downer) when it's an effort to even roll out of bed and straighten up. To "get with the program" takes some tall pulls on the boot straps. Often it seems everyone else in the world has had a good night's sleep, while we're still weary and bleary-eyed.

That's the time to make withdrawals on our Reserve Bank of built-up and saved-up philosophies and noble resolves...to accent the positive!

Let's face it: Those grandchildren and children we raised just aren't going to enjoy our company if we gripe about aches, pains, disagreeable weather and neighbors, and our loneliness.

Again, one of the best examples of this for me is my mother, who was widowed nearly all her life. After I was married and moved away, she prepared for long-term residence in an "empty nest" by filling her life with friends and hobbies and interests—and sticking to a sound, substantial philosophy that has stood the test of time. As a result, she is still independent and content.

She has often confided in me that when she was lonely and feeling sorry for herself when we didn't come to visit more often, she would get out of the house, go somewhere and do something for other people, then return home feeling that she was fortunate and blessed and happy to have her own comfortable home and health.

Her approach is an example for all of us: Get out and do something for others! It helps. And we'll come back to our quiet, "be-it-ever-so-humble" abode and feel truly that "there's no place like home."

There *are* times when we feel neglected and have occasion to think our children don't care about us,

✿ ✿ ✿

especially when we are "one" without a mate. Those are the times I use my mother's tricks of the trade. I invite the family (one or all) to visit, asking them over for dinner, a picnic, cake and pie, cookies, cinnamon rolls—just anything. I encourage you: **Take the initiative!**

Or, reach for the telephone and call them! Don't sit there depressed, feeling lower than a worm's heel as you wait for the telephone to ring. When you want to hear from them, *you* call *them!* If you decide you'd rather wait, you may wait a *l-o-n-g* time!

So go ahead and call, but don't spoil the contact by giving them a guilt complex as you express accusations about the absence of their attention to you. Like so many young families, they're probably so busy and into so many things that they don't have a clue you may be lonely and wanting to hear from them. Often it seems the younger generation is racing down the "fast lane" with high-octane blood in their veins while we're resting quietly by the side of the road, "thinking" too much.

You could view it as taking on the same attitude you had when you were courting—when you always had to smile and look your best, and put your best foot forward, and be charming and alluring enough to be sought after.

Be on your brightest behavior, and do some planning to help draw them to you so they'll *want* to come more often. Someday you may even be shooshing them away for coming too much.

✿ ✿ ✿

I get 'em one way or another. I *make* ways to get their attention and have them need me. For example, Spike and I live quite near our son Joe and his family, and I always keep a food cabinet supplied with things I know his wife Debbie Jo might run out of. She's learned about these provisions...so even if I don't get to be with her as much as I would like, I *know* she'll show up eventually to borrow something.

You have to outwit 'em, I figure. I've lived longer than they and know a lot more ways to skin a cat...so when I feel they're "outgrowing" us, I think up something else to bring them over.

Anyway, life is too precious to let it be spoiled by our getting down and depressed just because our children are too wrapped up in their own whirl of a world. Be independent! Keep blazing the trail of life! They'll get the message and come around with a case of curiosity just to see what it is you're so involved in. Admiration and attention will be bestowed upon you.

As parents and grandparents, our role continues until time takes its toll with us. That role means teaching and inspiring and *being*—who we are, where we are, how we are, and when we are.

Don't quit! As Precepts Bible study author and teacher Kay Arthur tells her students, "Hangest thou in there!"

✿ ✿ ✿

CHANGING TIMES

ONE OF THE BIGGEST challenges of grandparenting—be we fifty, sixty, or seventy—is facing up to "changing times" and all that they portend. Whether we're born and reared in the country or city-bred, we find that "things just ain't what they used to be." Communicating with and relating to kids is a whole new ballgame—EVERY DAY!

BUT the wondrous thing is that God's "things" and His truths don't waver one bit!

Watermelons still taste good and still produce more watermelon seeds. Oak trees still grow (slowly!) from acorns, and give shade. Crawdads may still be found (sometimes) under creek rocks, and some grapevines still support little folks who swing on them. Stones can still be skipped on the water after you learn just how to hold and throw them, and toadstools and mushrooms are as prevalent and mysterious as ever.

Cardinals and chickadees still stay year round at the birdfeeder while doves and finches come and go with the season. Squirrels try to rob birdfeeders like they always did, and put on a great show trying to do it.

Pigeon and duck company is still to be had for the feeding, and March (plus about six other months) is kite-time like always.

Carefully whittled or cobbled-up boats will still float on the pond or the creek, and get caught as usual in roots and rocks as they go with the flow or the wind, or are propelled by shoves from an impatient boy, girl, or old-timer.

Migrating geese and ducks over city or farm still know North from South, beckoning to be followed as they always have. Quail, field larks and pheasant are as startling as ever when they explode from their cover, and old eyes and young eyes strain to line up their landing place for the next big surprise.

Terrapins, it seems, just *must* cross the road; some make it, but some still get smushed, and that's bad. Snakes, too, often think the grass is greener; most of them make it across because they're faster than terrapins.

Shakespeare's "fickle moon" really isn't fickle at all, but still rises and sets right on time as it grows and shrinks. All that "changing times" have done to it is litter it up a bit with space travel junk, but big young eyes can't see it, much less old weary ones.

✳ ✳ ✳

The Evening Star still heralds another performance of the longest-running late show of all. As always that good ol' Big Dipper points to the North Star, and tells time, too, if you can stay awake that long.

Seasons change so predictably because God worked it all out a long time ago. Neither smog, nor greenhouse effect, TV or satellites change the schedule one bit.

A little child and his grandmother know that jonquils and violets portend spring with all its flower glory (both wild and tame), and the coming of birds and butterflies.

Summers are still for creek-freaks, river-runners, cannonballs and belly-floppers...except that "changing times" make it all easier at a water park than in the ol' swimming hole. (The ol' swimming hole, however, was probably more adventuresome, daring, and exciting.)

The wonder of fall, mysterious and unfathomable as the changing colors of the trees, is still a BIG DEAL that demands running and jumping into piles of leaves and packing them into poly bags. And winter (tough as it is on us comfort-lovers) still brings ice-sliding and snowballing, which are now more tolerable than in "olden times," what with garments made of Dacron II and Goretex.

New York's Central Park, Arizona's Grand Canyon, the Appalachians, the Ozarks, the Rockies, and all the vacant acres in between are a happy hunting-

✶ ✶ ✶

ground for God's great marvels and His little hidden secrets:

What's under a rock?
What's inside a hollow tree?
What's up the creek?
What's down the river?
How deep is a cave?
Where did the groundhog go?
When do beavers work?
How do robins find worms?

The answers are eternal...even in these "changing times."

Enjoy it all with your grandchild, and talk about it. As you take a walk in the woods, don't be intimidated because that smart little fellow—he's YOUR grandkid, you know—knows a lot more than you do about how purple finches find their way back to your woods each year, because he saw it on *Nova* or the *National Geographic* special. That isn't all bad... he needs to realize that grandparents don't know everything, and that maybe "a little kid can be right once in a while."

To younger grandparents, television—a boon or a curse of "changing times"—has "always" been here. But it may be a real intruder on family life, especially in the eyes of older grandparents. It can be a cop-out for us, or it can be an enhancer to story times and together-adventures. Since the parents of our grandchildren have pretty well set their family TV

* * *

ground-rules and habits, we must live with these rules, or at least use them as a starting place.

The competition in the grandparents' home between "quality talk time" and TV time can be a touchy issue. It may result in driving the grandkids home to sit in front of "their" TV and be in full control.

"Times" change so FAST nowadays. It used to be that a generation and its styles lasted twenty to thirty years. But now trends in apparel, music, real and imagined "national" heroes, pastimes and recreation are subject to seemingly weekly shifts, all at the dictate of the advertising gurus.

Keeping up and staying in touch has become almost impossible, but still imperative—and well worth the effort and really fun for all. Sometimes we find that the good old days really weren't all that good, and that the new eighteen-speed mountain bikes beat the heck out of our heavy old bikes and skate-mobiles.

While there is life, there is hope, and it's never too late to try new things, to stay in touch, and to keep current, even if we think most new music has dumb lyrics, and the latest dances are hard on old knees.

Times do change, and rapidly—but grandparents can change too, and be the happier and younger for it.

✶ ✶ ✶

Facts are facts, morals are fixed, tradition is great...but really, let's face it: We didn't have the final answers in our day, either!

★ ★ ★

WHEN YOU KNOW THE ANSWERS

 THIS PASSAGE by William Strawn is entitled *A Prayer for Older People* (and many grandparents are "older people"):

Father, Thou knowest
I am growing older. Keep me
from becoming talkative and
possessed with the idea that I must
express myself on every subject.
Release me from the craving
to straighten out everyone's affairs.
Keep my mind free from the recital
of endless detail. Seal my lips when I am
inclined to tell of my aches and pains.
Teach me the glorious lesson that
occasionally I may be wrong.
Make me thoughtful but not moody,
helpful but not bossy. With my vast store
of wisdom and experience, it seems a pity
not to use it all; but Thou knowest, Lord,
that I want to keep my friends
until the end.

Amen.

When I was in university administration we used to say that college sophomores thought they knew all the answers, but they just hadn't heard all the questions. **As we grow older we begin to think we, too, know all the answers...but sadly enough, no one asks us questions.**

As we watch our children learn the hard way to be parents, we wish they would ask us about almost every facet of child-raising. *We could save them so many headaches and heartaches,* we think. But they usually don't ask us until "after the fact," if then.

Wise grandparenting seems to be a matter of lots of looking, much listening, and constantly being available. "Constantly," that is, in a way that's consistent with our own balanced lifestyle.

A good approach seems to be summed up by grandparents saying, "In our house we'll do things like we always did (be it manners, meals, schedules, playing, or whatever), and we'll have fun doing it." Keeping it light and fun as you talk about a lifestyle in "our" house—which can be quite different from the lifestyle in "their" house—is the challenge. It doesn't always come out just right.

Authority must go with responsibility, and since, in most cases, the parents of our grandchildren have the responsibility for their kids, the parents' wants and wishes are pre-eminent. But grandparents can at least have the satisfaction of knowing they tried to communicate their perspective, stating their case by word or, even better, by unwavering example.

* * *

Our kids learned so much more from us by seeing what we did and how we lived, than they did by hearing what we said. And it must be so with our grandchildren. Kids are seldom fooled by phoniness and sham. They see right through to the heart and core of everything and everybody. Recognizing this clear-eyed perspective of theirs will help steer us to stronger relationships. The years make us older, but our thoughts, words, and deeds can provide us with a "younger touch" and a workable understanding of where kids are today.

An unforgettable line in the Broadway hit *West Side Story* came from the lips of the gang-leading "hero" in answer to a lovable old storekeeper who had said, "When I was your age..." The youth's response was, "Pop, you wuz never my age!"

That's absolutely right. There was a time, of course, when we were the same chronological age as our kids and their kids, but it was never in a time and place like they actually live in today.

Life may be the same jigsaw puzzle now as then, but the pieces are drastically different in size and shape. Our place is to help them work out the puzzle, if and when asked to do so.

We may think, as the "Prayer for Older People" expressed, that *with my vast store of wisdom and experience, it seems a pity not to use it all*—and that's so VERY TRUE. But our children and their children must *want* to hear it, and hopefully we will be available when they do want to.

✷ ✷ ✷

Sometimes, years later, they may say, "If I had just asked you, I know what the answer would have been ...and things would have turned out better."

A wise old friend of mine says, "When you are wrong, admit it, and when you are right, shut up." Great advice for grandparents, as well as parents... and people in general, young or old.

✶ ✶ ✶

HEROES

S INCE THE BEGINNING of time, our omnipotent God has used heroes (or "role models," as we call them now) to get His message across to all mankind about how He thinks life should be lived. There were the Exodus heroes, for example, who were God's follow-up—Moses, Joshua, and Caleb. And there were the heroic Old Testament prophets, Elijah, Jeremiah, Ezekiel, and the other forerunners and foretellers of Christ. The way they lived their lives was a monumental message. Likewise the message of Jesus Himself—and Paul's message, too—was more "See how I do it" than it was "Listen to what I say."

More than we know, we've had heroes who not only influenced our growing-up years, but also still shape our lives today, every day, all the way to the grave. Grandparents make natural "heroes" in this regard because, as my 95-year-old mother-in-law insists, "blood is thicker than water." Yes, we do tend to trust and believe more in "blood" than in other folks in general.

My mother was orphaned early in life so I never knew of or about her parents and heritage. But my dad's father was a folk hero to us all, though only by family legend. How brave and resourceful he was in leaving Wales on his own as a boy, landing in Minnesota, and finally coming to Texas and building a modest fortune. His story was regular fare at family reunions. We all knew that Grandfather always taught a Sunday school class of young adult men and kept in touch with all of them through family Sunday dinners in his home.

I have also been blessed beyond measure by having four other heroes in my life. Three of them, though not related to me by blood, served as pseudo-grandparents to me. One was a coach and a charter honoree in the Oklahoma Athletic Hall of Fame. Another hero was the pastor of the biggest congregation in Methodism. A third was dean of students at Texas A&M University.

The fact that one of these men was a hall of famer, one was a largest-church pastor, and one a university dean had little or nothing to do with my perception of them as heroes. There were other things about each man—things that go far beyond any worldly honors they received—that molded my life immeasurably, and **these qualities are exactly the things that make or break the images and memories kids have of grandparents.**

★ ★ ★

The coach, Bill Lantz, stayed at one high school for thirty-five years. He had opportunities to move up and out, but he knew his niche and filled it relentlessly. He was the best seven-days-a-week, 24-hours-a-day Christian I have ever known, and he was fun, fun, fun to be around, be it work or play. He never—repeat *never*—consumed any caffeine, any nicotine, any alcohol, or anything else that was harmful to his God-given body. He treated the bodily temple he lived in with disciplined respect as to exercise, food, rest, and recreation.

He never stopped thinking about his athletes and his friends, old and young—and also about what he perceived as God's plan for his life.

He never talked about any of the above; he just lived it. And we who watched could take it or leave it! Most of us took it and tried to emulate.

Besides his quality living, Coach Lantz also showed lifelong confidence in me and lifelong respect for my ideals and ideas. What an inspiring example for anyone, and particularly a grandparent!

The minister, Paul Quillian, epitomized a balanced lifestyle. In college he quarterbacked the football team, played the banjo, and sang with the best. He was so brilliant a student that he became an instructional department head at his alma mater at age twenty-five. His academic career was followed with great business success mixed with time for par golfing and extensive church involvement—which

✳ ✳ ✳

led to Christian seminary and the ministry. Paul Quillian had Class with a capital C.

Small wonder that when he showed concern and confidence in my career, I was impressed beyond measure and reacted with confidence. A grandfather to me?—no, but a hero and role model, absolutely.

Dean Penberthy was an all-time all-timer at Texas A&M University. His entire adult life was spent usefully in work for one great institution. During that time he was my boss and my friend. His entire purpose was friendship to student and faculty alike, and his career made a great university a cultural, social, and recreational hallmark.

By the mere fact that he believed in me and never failed to show his confidence and appreciation, I was inspired and stimulated.

My daddy was another of my heroes, though his only claim to fame was working hard, being a devoted father and husband, and having long-lasting good friends who respected his integrity, good humor, and camaraderie.

He can best be described as a good and humble man —he was always just that, no matter the circum-stances. His unfailing, ever-present, unceasing concern for me and my interests and efforts became a source of lifelong encouragement to me to do bigger and better.

✶ ✶ ✶

With the special link of blood kin, **grandparents can also be lifetime heroes.** How grandkids see us and what we show to them add up to the whole ball-game.

In a lifetime of working with kids, I have learned one great truth: **You can't kid a kid.** They KNOW real from fake, be it lifestyle or love. Assuming they look at us grandparents as heroes (and hero status has to be earned), their X-ray eyes and brains will evaluate our every move and motive, and these things will become a part of their make-up, good or bad.

Every member of the human race seeks approval and wants to be important. What better way for a child to grow secure and confident than to experience the admiration, love, and approval of a grandparent who really seems bigger than life?

✱ ✱ ✱

KEEP HOLDING
HANDS

O N AN AVERAGE SUMMER DAY in our resort town, some 25,000 visitors, give or take a few (and most times we'd rather "give" than "take"), come to see Silver Dollar City and other fun spots, as well as to experience music shows (nearly thirty of them), country crafts shops (more than I can count), and enticing eateries with Ozark vittles, funnel cakes, ice cream, fudge, pies, and more. It's all along a twelve-mile, two-lane stretch, and everyone going back and forth gives this entertaining town of ours a good case of congestion every summer.

Many of these vacationers are older couples, and among them, hand-holding is the *mode de jour.* I watch them sometimes when I go into town on an errand. Walking so intimately, they act like newlyweds all over again. Hand-in-hand they stroll in and out of the fudge shop, the ice cream parlor, the craft shops. They sometimes wear his-and-her shirts, and with the hand that isn't holding the other's hand, each of them is sharing the load of those packages of goodies and gifts for friends and family back home (tourist teamwork!). They're as close as our washer and dryer downstairs in the laundry room.

They buy those postcards of Ozarks hillbillies going out to the outhouse, going fishing, going on picnics, or just going to sleep under a shade tree in the middle of a summer day. They think that's the way we are, we who live here all year long. Of course, the postcards are made in New York or maybe California. And the visitors are sending them back home to New York or California, and writing on them, "Wish you were here."

They're having a good time...and they're holding hands! I wonder if they also hold hands back home and have fun together there, too.

It does seem to me that those of us who have made it this long in marriage *do* cling to one another more, and *do* care more. And I believe this is important for our grandchildren to realize in this world today, where broken marriages are so prevalent. They need to see their grandparents being affectionate and attentive to each other.

Just as Spike does, I enjoy B.J. Thomas's song, "Whatever Happened to Old-Fashioned Love?" If yours is an "old-fashioned love," show it! Live it! Pass it on! Advertise the product and prove its worth: "If you've got it, flaunt it!" Let the family see

✿ ✿ ✿

"how sweet it is," and maybe you can inspire them to emulate that affection and enjoyment in their own marriage.

And if your mate is no longer living, tell the grandchildren how precious your life was together. Tell them how you first met and about your courtship. Describe the best times and tell your best memories of your good life together.

Our grandgirls are often here when Spike comes home in the late afternoon, and they beat me to the door when they hear him drive up. They call out "Hi, Pappy!" and carry a cup of coffee or glass of ice tea ready to hand him. (They do that because they've seen me do it down through the years.)

After he comes in, we all sit down in a special place and talk: "Tell us, Pappy, what was so special today?" It's a ritual and tradition to talk together and to hear him tell of the day's activities while he has his "pick-up" before showering for supper.

All the while the girls are learning that Gran'maw makes a big "to do" over Pappy when he comes home. They see that their grandfather is king in this house, and that Gran'maw looks after him. To her, he's Numero Uno!

Often they've also seen how their Pappy—nearly every morning—writes little love notes to me and leaves them in special places where I can find them.

✿ ✿ ✿

"Old-fashioned love" is still alive and well in this family!

Hopefully, our grandchildren will grow up knowing that the relationship Spike and I enjoy is the way love and marriage should be, ideally—and they'll desire to have it in their lives, too.

I'm reminded of the reasoning expressed by the father of a boy who came to our camp. A friend asked him, "Isn't that a Christian camp your son attends each summer? I didn't know you were a Christian." He answered, "Oh well—I figure he's going to hear about it sometime, somewhere, anyway!"

As far as the beauty of "old-fashioned love" goes, your grandchildren may not "hear about it" from anyone else but you. So "show and tell!"

When all around you the affection of so many is waning...*keep holding hands.*

✿ ✿ ✿

OUR CHOICES

E TELL OUR grandkids that squirrels are squirrels because their mother was a squirrel and their dad was a squirrel; consequently, they have no choice but to be a squirrel. The same goes for frogs and turtles. Eggs are eggs, but if they were laid by an ostrich the eggs are monstrous, and in due time out comes an ostrich. Many snakes lay eggs, too, and if and when they hatch there are more snakes. Cowbirds will lay an egg in the nests of cardinals and other birds; when the unsuspecting cardinal hen (or Carolina wren, or whose ever nest has been infiltrated) hatches it, she has a cowbird to raise.

It is always that way, and always has been—no choices in the bird and animal world. Kids can understand that and see it daily.

To people, however, God gives choices—all day, every day, and all year, to the end of our days. We oldsters explain to children about choosing habits, choosing colleges, choosing mates, choosing professions, choosing to believe in God, and on and on.

Parents and grandparents get to choose, too. They have no choice in the sex of their children and often-times even the number of young'uns gets out of control, but what kind of parents and what kind of grandparents they will be is up for grabs!

Grandparents can choose to be aloof, distant, self-centered, and even unapproachable—or they can be handy, involved, available, generous, concerned... and loved. Most of us are probably somewhere in between, and that's not all bad, either.

With the wide variety in our lifestyles, economic sit-uations, geographic locations, and physical and mental health, there can be no "how to" directions or "add water and stir" prescriptions for successful grandparenting. But there's a lot we can think about to help us do it right.

All our Christian lives we've learned that "to give is to get," "to lose is to find," "use it or lose it," and "love is only love when you give it away." The choice is ours.

A home can be built and furnished with "comfort for two" the paramount concern—or it can be con-structed with "the more the merrier" in mind.

We can pack our schedules solid with all-adult and self-enrichment activities, or we can "Swiss-cheese"

* * *

those schedules with lots of time-holes for grandkids in particular and younger folks in general.

Our travel can be total comfort in luxurious "Geritol cruises" by bus or boat or plane, or it can be wild and loud and strenuous with family members of all ages involved.

Like most of life's great truths, balance is probably the answer to all the above. Surely older couples deserve and need time just to themselves, to enjoy the lifetime relationship they have built. But for pure unadulterated FUN, we'll take the "younger the better" most of the time, with well-deserved rest in between.

The degree of involvement we choose in our grandkids' lives will be directly proportional to the love and respect we will receive from them. Seniority itself does not produce love, and though we feel it should be automatic, respect also has to be earned. Gratitude and expressed appreciation from our grandchildren may be a long time surfacing, but grandparents can wait, and eventually our investment of time and love pays off—and may even be recognized and praised.

When it comes down to it, our many choices between possible instant reward and long-term payoff are not really that hard to make—when true *value* is uppermost in our judgment.

✶ ✶ ✶

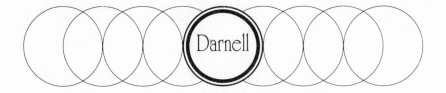

SIMPLE FUN

W HEN OUR BOYS were young, the television reception in our small college town left much to be desired, but we thought we had a goldmine in the living room: everything from Howdy Doody and Uncle Miltie to Hit Parade and Dragnet.

We were hard up, but we didn't know the difference.

One daytime program the boys always watched featured a Miss Frances. Miss Frances was a sweet lady who could charm any child from one to six (she's probably the person who taught Barbara Walters and Dale Carnegie how to win friends and influence people). She was also a genius; she never raised her voice and never repeated a direction, but the kids would be mesmerized. That meant moms could get the washing washed and hung out to dry, as well as the mopping and cooking done while Miss Frances worked her magic.

The kids could be heard actually carrying on conversations with her. She coolly asked questions of them, and I'll swear she had radar eyes and ears that could take in their responses through the television screen. She knew when they would answer, and she and they talked back and forth.

That lady had class! And she showed respect to mothers! She ended her program with, "Now go get your mother and ask her to come and let me talk to her." Mothers would obediently and immediately drop the wash basket on the grass, or leave the pudding to scorch on the back burner, or walk away from the shirt being ironed, and dash into the living room to see what Miss Frances wanted.

She usually was very generous, and let us moms in on the trick of making all those neat sailboats, valentines, masks, turkeys, and other *objets d'art.* She made my day by allowing me to join in the inner sanctum of the wonder world she shared with the kids. And I found that Miss Frances and I could talk together, too. I always answered her: "Yes" or "No," or "Oh yes, I will," and "Thank you, Miss Frances!"

Now I lie awake nights wondering whatever happened to Miss Frances. I'm certain she is out there somewhere being idolized by a mess of grandkids and great-grandkids. Or perhaps she is wearing the coveted Crown of Crayons in heaven.

This talented lady's example stayed with me as I moved from motherhood to grandmotherhood. I

✿ ✿ ✿

found a book that helped make a pseudo Miss Frances out of me, and I studied it and used it with my grandchildren when they were small. The book is *Holiday Magic,* published by Doubleday. I'm sure there are dozens like it and maybe better, but this one served to make me look good while entertaining the children and teaching them fun projects.

I also learned that volunteering to help occasionally at a preschool is not all that tough—in fact, it's educational and enlightening. It's a sneaky and cheap way to learn more new projects that make me look and feel as savvy and awesome as Miss Frances!

In other chapters and the "Scrapbook" sections you'll see more of what I've learned about how to be winsome with grandkids. For now I'll just say that one of the most important things I've learned is this: **Make the most of *simple fun.***

After all, you have to be pretty simple to be a good grandparent—and I am simple.

✿ ✿ ✿

YOUR GREATEST SERVICE

I N AUTUMNS PAST, once the fall colors were over, our Ozark vacation paradise would usually pull down the shades and settle down for a long winter's nap. Then along in April and May the town becomes wide-eyed and bushy-tailed, rarin' to receive the thousands-a-day tourists who seem to like it here in "our town."

Last year, however, the merchants collectively agreed to keep the red carpet rolled out for visitors until Christmas—a "first" for us—and to treat the tourists to a real Ozark Christmas gala. It was quite a show! The motel sign stayed lighted up —"No Room In The Inn"— through December, and cars were bumper-to-bumper on West 76 until the end of the year. In Silver Dollar City, Mary's Park glittered and sparkled with thousands upon thousands of little lights, like a fairyland in a Disney production, or Rockefeller Center during the holidays. We looked *good!*

The Shepherd of the Hills outdoor-theater crew closed the season with a grand finale, the piece de resistance. It was a production of the classic *How Come Christmas?* with skilled actors, a marvelous script, and excellent scenery and costumes. There were chariots racing back and forth (with the Ozarks in the background), plus horses, sheep, camels, and a proud donkey for Mary to ride.

One line in the play was provocative to me, and I've thought about it a great deal. Mary was close to "term" in her pregnancy, and she and Joseph were ready to leave for the long, rough sojourn to Bethlehem. As the couple departed, Mary's mother was apprehensive and fearful and called out sadly and wearily to her daughter on the donkey: "I'll pray for you!" She was praying for her grandson-to-be—for *Jesus!* (Doesn't that send icy fingers up and down your spine?)

It occurred to me that during the times when we as grandparents cannot be "on location" to serve our children and grandchildren physically, we can always do what may well be the most important service—to *pray* for them.

Our family is like other families: We have had heartaches and disappointments, including divorce —although in my eyes and Spike's, divorce is a stigma. Our philosophy is, "You stick with things you start, and master them... Don't give up!"

But we can't live our children's lives and are never given that opportunity anyway. When marriages are

✿ ✿ ✿

dissolved, all you can do in the overall picture is *listen,* and *love* and *pray.* What goes on "behind the green door" will remain a mystery that we are not allowed to share.

Knowing that God is sovereign, I find that His strength carries me between the rock and the hard places! I realize He is in control, and I turn everything over to Him to help us all. I just wonder: How do folks make it when these hard experiences and trials come their way if they do not call upon their Lord for guidance?

My nature is to avoid the bad and the ugly. I'm like an ostrich, prone to hide my head in the sand when the going gets tough and I can't compete or control or connect with it. That's when I become the biggest "tattler" on earth: I tattle everything to the Lord. I know He hears when I pray, and that's the way I handle my troubles when it isn't in "my territory" per se. And oh, how I pray!

In a recent edition of the little daily devotional magazine *Our Daily Bread* was an account of a great-grandmother who had thirty-seven great-grandchildren and who knew each one by name. When asked by a friend how she remembered them all, she answered, "I know them all because every night I pray for each one by name." How blessed to be a grandparent or a great-grandparent like that!

Paul, in 2 Timothy 1, writes of the godly influence of Timothy's grandmother Lois. Doubtless she prayed daily for her grandson.

✿ ✿ ✿

And I guarantee there are grandmothers and grand-
fathers today who are also doing some tall talking to
God (and trusting of God) for their grandchildren.
The granddaddy I sleep with has callouses on his
knees from praying long and lovingly for all of us.
That man has a red line to heaven; he does some
major praying!

Susannna Wesley, so incredibly busy with her
nineteen children (among whom were Charles
Wesley and John Wesley), found time in the middle
of her days to pray. In the kitchen she would just
gather up the hem of her apron, cover her head, and
pray. It must have worked for her.

I recall the story of a grief-stricken boy at his grandfather's funeral. The young boy was asked, "Has
your grandfather's death changed you?" The boy
replied, "No, my grandfather's *life* changed me."

**How many of *us* can say, "I have made a differ-
ence"?**

The way we pray can mean that difference in our
children's and our grandchildren's lives, as well as
in our own. So take up the sword...and be a prayer
warrior! Our grandchildren need our prayers—
perhaps even more than we know.

✿ ✿ ✿

THE
ANSWER

WE ALL PRAY for inspiration, guidance, forgiveness, and heavenly triumph, and the older and wiser we get the more fervently we pray. An added blessing is spending prayer time taking inventory of our grandchildren as to condition and position. In this day of frequent family breakups and family moves, stressful pursuits for higher education and happiness and many other things, and young folks' search for independence, a regular daily "inventory assessment" is needed.

Thoughtful and unhurried prayer about grandkids is almost as satisfying as "reaching out and touching." In the process, a mix of Divine inspiration and grandparental love produces wonderful ideas and game plans for closer walks in the future, as well as memories of the past.

A pen and pad on the night table can be a big help to short memories, because we all know that God-given ideas and inspiration may come anytime, and proper results may be instant as well as long-term.

One of our very best longtime friends whose children and grandchildren are in big trouble seems to receive frequent glimpses of "the rest of the story" through fervent prayer. These assurances bolster her faith immeasurably, and fortify her spirit.

In our influence on our grandkids' maturity and wisdom and character, any and every grandparent is really just "buying time" from the Lord until the brain growth in those kids catches up with their bodily growth, and their judgment catches up with the horsepower of their current vehicle. Growing up is an "iffy" game nowadays, and kids need all the help they can get, whether they know it or not. We all know about God's plan in general, but learning the details is much more fun and comforting as we mortals who happen to be grandparents try to pray our way through our roles.

Grandparental prayer is not the whole solution, but it sure does provide a lot of answers and inspiration. Besides, when praying for them we can't be accused of "interfering" in the kids' lives, because only God knows.

A child who is prayed for 365 days a year, for however many years of life, is bound to be on God's "TO DO" list. That's a lot of praying by the time that grandchild gets grown.

✷ ✷ ✷

It doesn't take satellite systems, conference calls, or charge cards to reunite. Prayer pulls it off—whether we or they are in mangrove hummocks in Deep South swamps, or snow camps on the Bering Sea. From a hang-glider's heights in a country sky to a diver's depths off a barrier reef...**prayer is the answer.**

* * *

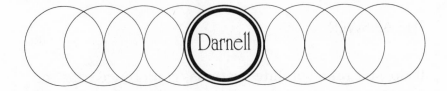

IMPORTANT— & AVAILABLE

RANDPARENTS OUGHT TO BE like oatmeal: long-lasting...satisfying... stick-to-your-ribs...filling you up!

I attend a Precepts Bible study class once a week, a class taught by our daughter-in-love, Debbie Jo. (Being taught so ably is a real plus in my life!) The class is made up of about twenty-five young, attractive, intelligent women. Believe me, I have to get up by dawn's early light to keep up with these gals—they set a pace that keeps me "hup-two-ing." My life has been sharpened and enriched from their earnestness and devotion.

Very few of them haven't at some time or another said to me, "I wish our children had their grandmother as near as Debbie Jo does. I miss that so much for them and for us. Our children are growing up without that special ingredient!"

How many times have you heard grandparents say (or said it yourself?), "Frankly, we've lived our lives for our kids, and now we're going to live for ourselves"? They've moved to a condo in Winter Park or Scottsdale or some remote hideaway...hidden away, all right, from the days of houses filled with happy children's voices and home-cookin' smells. They're all alone now in their new environs—and one day that's just what they'll realize they are: *alone!*

Of course, to be near our loved ones we don't have to just "hang around" all the time and be in the way, causing our children to resent us for trying to run their lives. It *is* important—for us as well as for them—to make our own friends, have our own social life, and "do our own thing."

But—will we be near enough and stay long enough to be available when really needed, and to truly fill the unique role of a grandparent?

Occasionally, when I make telephone calls from my office, a voice on the other end of the line answers like this, "I'm sorry, Mr.____ *is not available;* if you will leave your name and number, he will get back to you." (And of course, sometimes Mr.____ does, and sometimes he doesn't.)

Wouldn't you just die (pardon the pun) if that message was the epitaph your survivors chose for your grave marker?

NOT AVAILABLE—
NOW, OR IN LIFE

✿ ✿ ✿

I believe the key to making yourself appropriately available to your children's children is to realize an all-important truth: **You are important in the recipe of building your grandkids' lives—and don't ever think you aren't!**

You are important!

Grandparents are needed not only to encourage one another, but also to encourage their grandchildren, as well all the other young people we have contact with.

The truth of the matter, of course, is that *everyone* is important. Not long ago, Ann Landers ran this clever item in her newspaper column:

> Dear Readers: What you are about to read was sent to me by a reader from Tennessee. No sign of the author, sorry to say.
>
> This little essay drives home the point, in a forceful manner, that each of us is an important part of a bigger picture.
>
> Keep this handy and reread it when you get to feeling insignificant. You DO count. And if you doubt it, read this a second time.

AM I REALLY NEEDED?

```
Xvxn though my typxwritxr is an old
modxl, it works wxll xxcxpt for onx
of thx kxys. I'vx wishxd many timxs
that it workxd pxrfxctly. Trux, thxrx
```

❀ ❀ ❀

arx 42 kxys that function, but onx
kxy not working makxs thx diffxrxncx.

Somxtimxs it sxxms to mx that our
organization is somxwhat likx my
typxwritxr — not all thx pxoplx arx
working pxrfxctly. You might say,
"Wxll, I'm only onx pxrson. It won't
makx much diffxrxncx." But you sxx,
an organization, to bx xfficixnt,
nxxds thx activx participation of
xvxry pxrson.

Thx nxxt timx you think your
xfforts arxn't nxxdxd, rxmxmbxr my
typxwritxr, and say to yoursxlf, "I
am a kxy pxrson, and thxy nxxd mx
vxry much."

✿ ✿ ✿

DOLLARS
& DECISIONS

A NEW CHECKBOOK is so exciting. It just lies there so crisp and clean, waiting to be used or abused, ready to unfold adventure and opportunity, or pampering and spoiling.

Many of us, by the time we're grandparents, have (to use a popular phrase) "discretionary income." That checkbook represents our freedom to unlock either paradise or Pandora's box.

The older we get the greater the dilemma of deciding how much to save (for taking care of our unproductive and perhaps catastrophic days) and how much to use now and see it enjoyed. We've all chuckled to see the luxurious travel camper tooling down the interstate highway toward the sunset, with a bumper sticker that proclaims, WE ARE SPENDING OUR CHILDREN'S INHERITANCE.

Who knows the proper balance between generosity, wisdom, conservatism, and self-preservation? And who knows where to draw the line between those qualities on the one hand, and ostentation, egotism, and bribery on the other?

"If not applicable, read no further," as the question-naires say. But really, whether your financial means are large or little, as a grandparent the question is always there to some degree: whether to "spoil or ignore" your grandchildren. The grandmother who "always gave us candy" guaranteed sweet memories but may have ruined a lot of teeth and appetites.

The Bible doesn't say *money* is the root of all evil, but rather the misuse and love of money. Likewise our federal government offers evidence time after time that money by the billions cannot solve all the problems, and often creates worse ones.

So what to do, as we see our years winding down and our interest on CDs growing?

Long-range, realistic, "worst scenario" planning can secure both the financial independence of the grand-parents as well as the availability of funds for the grandkids, either directly or through their parents.

What are the opportunities? Here are some to consider:

* Seed money for education and recreation provides great benefit to the recipient and pleasure to the donor. A half-and-half

✴ ✴ ✴

approach—the grandparents matching the amount earned by the grandchild—can be an incentive to him or her, as well as a way out for you if plans or circumstances change.

Family legends passed on by my uncles and aunts tell of wise decisions by those who parlayed grandparental educational funds into lifetime professional careers, and perpetuated similar generosity down through the generations.

* "Three-generational travel" (with you picking up the tab) means family togetherness beyond measure. The only return the grandparent may get is a group picture, but that picture provides unending assurance of money well-spent.

* Expansion of homes for rapidly growing families sometimes just can't be pulled off by family income alone, but can be hastened by the grandparents' partial underwriting.

* Modern teenagers seem to literally live for the day when they can finally get their driver's license and own their very own "wheels." Most times, however, the wheels are about all they can afford. What an opportunity the acquisition of their first car can provide a grandparent to help or hinder in this loved teenager's exciting and fast-forming life. Then the question becomes: Something shiny and fast and new, or something well-used but still repairable. There's no pat answer, and like

✶ ✶ ✶

most solutions, the best answer probably lies somewhere in between. The big benefit is that grandparents "cared and shared" in the problem and in the solution.

"Discretionary" dollars can also be used for character training. We all remember the vintage story of the grandmother who gave her college-bound grandson a new Bible before he left home. At her urging, the "plebe" promised her he would read it every day. When he came home at Christmas, she asked if he had kept his promise, and he assured her he had done as he had vowed.

Wise in the ways of the young, the grandmother opened up the Bible, turned to Second Chronicles, and took out the undiscovered fifty-dollar bill she had placed there months before. To the chagrin and astonishment of her grandson, she then placed the bill in her purse.

We can't be sure the incident led the grandson to daily Bible reading, but I'm sure it taught him not to lie to his grandmother.

Just as King Richard exulted, "I like being king," so we grandparents can say, "I love being a grandparent"—then adding, "especially when I have some bucks to bounce around!"

* * *

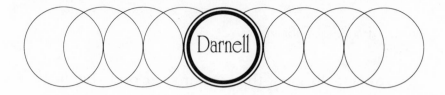

IT TAKES A HEAP OF LIVIN'...

OME DEFINITIONS in my *American Heritage Dictionary* for **heap:** "to fill to overflowing; pile up; a great deal; lots."

We must "pile up" the love and laughter and life in our grandchildren any and every time we have (or can make) the opportunity.

I've read that the first three to five years of a child's life are the most important. Spending patient and loving time in those years training, disciplining, and caring for a child in consistent and regular routines—all this is part and parcel in the "heap of living" it takes to make a child well-adjusted and happy.

In years past, most parents raised and trained their children in the same way they themselves were trained, and they had continuing help from their own parents and grandparents. But now so many people are living away from the guidance and advice and supervision of the generations before them.

So much has changed—new lifestyles, different attitudes. "We've come a long way, Baby!" We remember when there were no X- or R-rated movies (or even PG's, which keep in four-letter words and "take the Lord's name in vain"). There was no "gay rights" movement and no teenage drug problem, and the top-selling prescription drug wasn't a tranquilizer. Prayer, Bible reading and the Pledge of Allegiance weren't banned from the schools. The power of parental guidance wasn't dilluted by the influence of television, and there weren't so many working mothers who had decreased the amount of time spent with their children in those preschool formative years, so important in a child's growth.

Well—enough of getting morbid. It's probably no more productive than our remembering when gasoline was thirteen cents a gallon and a quart of milk the same. As Walter Cronkite might say, "And that's the way it *was.*"

So we start with *here* and *now* and do something to counteract any bad vibes, and keep heaping on good ones. After all, there are so many lovely things to instill in our grandchildren.

Spike has written here about his "heroes" and I have mine also. Of those I've read about and admire, my

✿ ✿ ✿

list of the top three would include Mother Teresa (isn't she at the top of everyone's list?), Ruth Bell Graham, and Helen Hayes.

Another hero is Susanna Wesley, for the way she raised her nineteen(!) children. Her husband and children rose up and called her blessed, and so do I! Imagine raising nineteen children—and without a washer and dryer, dishwasher, or indoor plumbing.

Besides working the family farm, teaching Bible classes, and conducting her children's elementary education at home (which a number of young mothers are also doing today), the most amazing item in Susanna Wesley's list of accomplishments is that she disciplined herself to spend an hour alone with each of her children every week.

Spike and I can vouch for the wisdom and merits of giving undivided attention to a child individually. This is so worthwhile in every family when there is more than one child.

Providing that kind of special attention for kids is something we grandparents can take upon our-selves. It's a big part of the heaping on of living and love and training of each grandchild, whenever and however we can. There *are* ways to do it, even when we can't be as close to our grandchildren as we would like.

I often tell one of the grandchildren, "You are a pretty good kid for a grandkid!" That grandchild *knows* I think he or she is special!

✿ ✿ ✿

I'll close this chapter with reminders from the Bible about God's desire and plan for seeing these children grow into maturity, and especially for their growth in knowing and obeying God's Word:

> "*Train a child in the way he should go,* and when he is old he will not turn from it."
>
> (Proverbs 22:6)

> "See, I have taught you decrees and laws as the LORD my God commanded me... Watch yourselves closely so that you do not forget the things your eyes have seen or let them slip from your heart as long as you live. *Teach them to your children and to their children after them...*"
>
> (Deuteronomy 4:5,9)

> "These commandments that I give you today are to be upon your hearts. *Impress them on your children.* Talk about them when you sit at home and when you walk along the road, when you lie down and when you get up."
>
> (Deuteronomy 6:6-7)

Grandparents: We have our work cut out for us!

✿ ✿ ✿

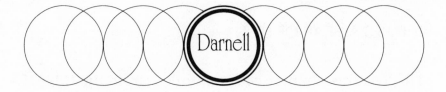

THIS GUY SPIKE

S PIKE IS the epitome of an all-around neat and complete grandfather, though he doesn't have an inkling that he is. He's just lived this way all his life. How-To lessons could be taken by simply observing him.

Our daughters-in-love would be the first to sing his praises—to tell you that Spike is always "there" when all else fails...when a good friend is needed. In his unobtrusive way he is like the proverbial godmother waving a magic wand. Such a gentle man, always serving and comforting and encouraging.

Grandchildren of all ages adore him for his story-telling and originality. He is half-eccentric and half-nomadic. We all marvel at his energy and enthusiasm.

This grandfather is fascinating to the family and a favorite topic. "Gran'maw, where is Pappy? What's he up to now?"

Spike "thinks up" and builds rope courses, obstacle courses, the "world's longest and fastest" water slides, ziplines to whiz down cliffs a hundred feet high, and rope-climbing towers to practice rappeling...all so the campers can have adventures in the summertime.

When he isn't working on a project for "kids," he is off running rivers—though in his seventies, he is an active kayaker. Last year he rounded out the "ten best rivers" in the United States for kayaking. A two-week run of the Grand Canyon's Colorado River was a highlight!

One of his yuppie friends who was there sent me a picture showing Spike, having just finished running the Lava and Son of Lava rapids, being picked up, still in his kayak, and paraded around the sandbar as a victor triumphant! Majestic precipices on either side completed the picture of splendid pomp and ceremony.

Spike often gets mail from his young "fresh-air friends" across the country, inviting him to join in another exciting adventure. As Mark Twain put it, "He is a good man to run a river with."

The Outward Bound organization awarded Spike a certificate with this personal message attached: "You are the oldest (by ten years!) person to have taken a course at NCOBS. You will always be an inspiration to all OBers. May you always remain as young as you are."

✿ ✿ ✿

The certificate reads:

Awarded in testimony of personal commitment,
perseverance, and selflessness demonstrated
in meeting the challenges
of OUTWARD BOUND

No wonder grandkids love and admire their Pappy!

He teaches them and sets before them the exciting adventure of aspiration. Already three grandsons have gone to Nantahala Outdoor Center for kayaking courses, and now they all have kayaks and run the rivers. Granddaughter Jamie Jo is next in line and is raring to go to NOC this year with her Pappy. And what granddad has a grandson booking him for Easter Break to run a Class 4 and Class 5 river! Scott, a student at Baylor University, telephones Spike often to river-talk and "plan for the next one."

Hang-gliding is the latest activity Spike has undertaken. He did admit that his legs don't move as fast as they used to, and getting off the ground to glide wasn't easy...but he is still hanging in there and soaring!

His philosophy: There's nothing to it but to do it, so try it.

This granddad is awesome! We all love him and admire his courage and individuality. He knows "when to hold 'em and when to fold 'em."

✿ ✿ ✿

And when Spike talks, we all listen! He is never without a story, and we're always ready to hear one. In fact, this raconteur is sometimes too verbal. If I'm in a hurry and want to know something from him, I have learned to preface the question with, "Spike, just answer Yes or No..."

Spike has a degree in electrical engineering, and when he was a young graduate and I first dated him, my friend Sara June said, "I'd rather marry an Eagle Scout than an engineer any day." But Spike was an Eagle Scout, too, so I felt secure. In fact, Spike personifies the Boy Scout oath, "On my honor I will do my best..."

As a friend to kids, a friend to friends, a grandfather, a father, and a husband...this guy is fun to have around.

✿ ✿ ✿

NO PLACE LIKE HOME
(except Gran'maw's)

MY BEST GIRLFRIEND of fifty-three years still answers to "Hey, Baby!"… but many more call her "Gran'maw." The littlest grandchild (a new step-grand-daughter, Brandi) calls her "Gran'mawwhite" (all one word).

The sign on her doorway says,

> THERE'S NO PLACE LIKE HOME…
> EXCEPT GRAN'MAW'S.

Here, for her, life is and has always been her kids and their kids. Whether it's playing table games at a card table that's always up and ready, sewing special-occasion dresses, tending the bean pot and cornbread oven, or knocking out long, interesting, fun letters to all the family, Gran'maw makes sure that her house is for kids, old or young!

As is true in most any other Gran'maw's house —whether it's a squeezed-in track home on a

50'x150' city lot, a rambling log home in the woods, or something in between—it bursts every eave and rafter with kid corners and memory-makers.

Let me say more about that house for you...and perhaps you'll see that I'm describing your house as well.

A porch swing on the back side is where Gran'maw always has time "to listen," or where little girls can swing alone just to have time to be free from grown folks and to dream girl dreams.

A small closet just for dolls and all their fixings becomes a private world and an escape hatch from the ordinary—as make-believe becomes the real world, and that little girl dreams her way into it.

A bay window seat set off by a draw curtain becomes a solarium and a private overlook upon the outside world, with the child's choice to take it or leave it.

Shelves of trip mementos stir adventurous memories for young and old; they demand long and not-so-long stories about faraway people and places, and hopefully stir an interest in the world "over there."

Birdfeeders outside the breakfast room windows provide a changing panorama of old feathered friends and new. Whether perching or hanging, bathing or drinking, pecking or playing, the show goes on. Gran'maw has time to keep the suet, sand, seeds, and kernels in their expected places, and

✶ ✶ ✶

always knows the bird names and habits, where they go when they're gone—and when they'll be back—and (excuse the pun!) the birds' family tree. (Grandparents seem so wise to grandkids who absorb from them such fascinating information.)

The rugged-but-right toy box in the hallway is so much a sign of stability because it always has those same toys and games and soldiers and forts in mostly the same places. Space to spread out is handy at Gran'maw's house, and things can stay out till play is over. Gran'maw's very own electric train pulls out from under furniture, and is always ready to run among the little block houses and stations.

The ping-pong table is always up and ready— unless, of course, some adult took it down to play pool. But then, pool is a good game for little folks, too, if there are short cues and long bridges to hold, and platforms to stand on and shoot from.

Gran'maw always has nice green grass in her yard— and hopefully some bare spots too, so little cars and trucks and draglines and backhoes can perform, by push or by remote control. The appeal of sand to all ages is just as strong in the backyard sandpile as it is on Waikiki—and it's a whole lot handier and more private.

Things are always in the same place. The same songbooks and sheet music are always on the piano, and the old favorite piano rolls are stacked on top of the player piano. The kazoos and mouth harps are handy, too, for hum-alongs. The closet under the

★ ★ ★

stairs is bursting with old-timey straw hats, dresses and coats for shows and talent contests to accompany the rinky-tink and honky-tonk piano roll music.

A pull-down silver screen and handy slide projector and movie machine put home movies, travel slides, and nature pictures at fingertip level. Videos add to the fun if carefully selected and if time allows.

Outside in the off-season closets are stored sleds, sleep-out tents, camping gear, scuba gear, and yard tools sized for large and small. Kayaks, canoes, and bikes hang handy and in the dry.

The firewood—neatly stacked and handy for hauling —tells the child of drought and rain, hard wood and soft, green wood and dry. And the kindling box is a treasure trove for boards to make boats, bridges, fences, highways, traps, and, of course, shacks and cave covers. The only other ingredient needed is a little imagination.

Nearby are hollow logs, woodpeckered trees, twisted driftwood, and Indian rocks almost covered with English ivy, which hangs from the eaves and the leaning trees.

Gran'maw's may not be a zoo, but it seems that there is always a big friendly dog, several not-so-friendly squirrels, a bashful chipmunk, a few frogs, and a few thousand frog eggs in the pond near the house. Crows are in the trees checking on everything. And if you are real lucky, occasionally a deer or a turkey will come by. Coons seldom are seen

✷ ✷ ✷

except at night, but leave their track and tooth marks to be sleuthed out.

Of course, there are other homes that have all the stuff Gran'maw's house has—but the difference is that Gran'maw goes with it. She plays, applauds, teaches, watches, listens, understands, and—most important of all—is just there.

Make no mistake: To small fry and big, there's no place like home...except Gran'maw's.

✶ ✶ ✶

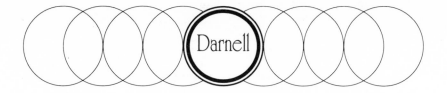

NIGHT & DAY

PIKE AND I are the fortunate ones when we get to have any of the grand-children all to ourselves without their parents. Then we can "do our own thing" and settle down to real livin' without review from the critics.

That's when you feel the ole' shriveled heart gets back its greenness.

The best times (especially when they come one at a time) are when the grandchildren spend the night, or come to "stay a while."

Cody, the older brother in his family, came to visit us frequently when his four-year-old brother Wesley developed diabetes and was a patient at Barnes Children's Hospital in St. Louis. (Wesley was very sick, and his wonderful mother and daddy went through months of suffering and heartaches, longing for Wesley's healing and restoration to a normal life. His mother faithfully and devotedly spent the months in the hospital caring for him, and became a solace to other mothers with children in similar situations.)

As grandparents we were needed to take care of Cody, and he stayed with us several weeks at a time. We were blessed to have this dear lad so near to us.

Each night as we retired, we had wonderful and intimate talks that can only be had when the lights are off and you are lying in the dark, being quiet and close together.

I asked him every night the same question: "Cody, what was the best thing that happened to you today?" (First, however, I asked Spike the question, thus setting precedence for a positive and happy answer. Spike would, of course, have some wonderful and winning story of the day's gift to him, then he would usually address the question to me. By this time Cody would be eager to play the game and to respond.)

Since then, asking that question has been the pattern for when a grandchild spends the night with us. This is an infectious way to end the day. It stretches the child's awareness and makes him aware of the good things that have happened to him that day. He forgets all the unpleasantness, home-sickness, and fears, if any, and drops off to a sweet sleep.

A while back, in a magazine review of Steve Allen's twenty-ninth book, *Adventures in the Vast Waste-*

✿ ✿ ✿

land, I read of a similar night-time ritual. Allen recalls it as...

> "...something I picked up years ago from Sam Goldwyn, Jr., who told me that almost every night, when he tucked his daughter into bed, he would say to her, "By the way, sweetheart, in case the question ever comes up in future years, you ARE having a happy childhood."

✿ ✿ ✿

THE
HOTLINE

C OLLECT OR PAID, local or long distance, emergency or social...the Grandma & Grandpa Hotline is always open (or has an alternate number).

Grandkid calls may be prompted by too steamy a date, a sudden thunderstorm, an empty gas tank or a carburetor malfunction, lack of credit at McDonald's, a fender-bender, or an encounter with the police.

Sometimes the caller wants to talk to his parents and tell them all about it — *but not right now.* In the meantime, a call to grandparents can buy time to think, as well as calm troubled waters and allow the kid to get on safer turf.

Sometimes the call is a plea for a ride to or from a friend's house, or to do some "absolutely important shopping." Sometimes the call is from the school gym after an extra long practice (it's comforting and convenient for the "shuttle bus driver" to know the area, and just what streetlight to look under.) Sometimes the call entails an "ambulance run" when the school nurse can't locate the parents, and a sick child needs home more than school that day.

The hotline to our house has an answering machine, and the name of it is Gran'maw. Often when a grandkid's request comes over the line, the Gran'maw Machine activates and expedites "all hands" and available vehicles (most often, Pappy and his four-wheel-drive pickup).

Hotline habits don't just happen. **Confidence is established over a lifetime by the grandparents' availability, patience, understanding, and proven action.** All of us—and especially kids—want instant answers and quick relief, and grandparents are almost always there, if not in person then at least by phone. Everyone needs to be needed, and a handy-dandy hotline is the handle for the wide-ranging, ever-increasing life circles that our grandkids are growing up in.

Our hotlines may have hearing aids and slow reactions and wake-up time, but to grandkids, availability and access count for a lot when the going gets tough and Murphy's Law has taken over.

Whatever the situation or setting, established and proven grandparent hotlines are, as the kids say, "action awesome."

★ ★ ★

HELLO?...IS THAT YOU, MYRT?

I 'll be the first to stand up and holler when they say, "Let's hear it for Dr. Alexander Graham Bell!"

BUT...overall, his telephone has stifled and supplanted an important and intimate communication.

Now, I'm as guilty as the folks next door of "reaching out and touching someone" fairly often—but whatever happened to the unequaled art of letter writing? Ralph Emerson must be turning over in his grave every time family members telephone each other instead of writing.

By comparison to the telephone, letters are hands-down more satisfying in getting news and information. When we talk to one of our children's households, each of their telephones has someone listening and trying to say something, all at once. "Hi, how are you?" "Who is this?" "What's been happening?" "What's that?" "Who am I talking to?"

Usually I'm talking to Spike—who's on the other phone in *our* house —telling him what some timid, tender-voiced person is mumbling that Spike can't hear.

We all talk as if we were nincompoops, leaving each other dangling like participles. "Thanks for calling...I love you!" "Good-bye!"

And that's it. Hearing their voices was nice, but we still know hardly a thing more than when we dialed.

The absolute worst is calling our kin across the Great Divide and hearing one of those "answering machine messages." I am so intimidated by the time the "sound of the tone" sounds, that I am almost speechless, and I leave idiotic and juvenile messages in a voice that I myself wouldn't recognize as my own.

Invariably I hang up frustrated and unfulfilled, resigned and vowed to make a list of "messages" so I can be prepared next time I have to talk to a machine.

My list would look something like this:

- ❀ (In song:) "I Just Called to Say, 'I Love You' " (thanks to Stevie Wonder).
- ❀ "I wish you had told me you aren't there; this is costing me money!"

❀ ❀ ❀

✿ "We are moving to the Rain Forest."

✿ "When did you get so organized? You were never this way when you lived at home."

✿ "This is your MOTHER! I HATE talking to a dummy!"

✿ "I've been kidnapped by a band of Gypsies! They are holding me for ransom."

✿ "I've forgotten why I called you."

✿ ✿ ✿

ADVENTURE TRAVEL

GRANDPARENTS COME in all sizes and shapes and, of necessity, in all income levels from mega-rich to subsistence living. Fortunately, however, there's no fixed price tag on "adventure."

Pardner, my wife's 95-year old mother (and the great-grandmother of our grandchildren), tells of "adventure camping" in deep East Texas when her own parents and grandparents and aunts and uncles packed a wagonload of watermelons, a wagonload of live chickens, and a wagonload of cousins piled on bedding galore, and all went to the river for a two-week vacation of fishing, swimming, playing, tree-climbing, and probably mosquito-swatting. Adventure? YOU BET!!

We all know about family adventures to Disney World or Disneyland or Aspen or Maui, but most kids would just as soon drift down a slow-moving river in a canoe or a johnboat, getting out to play when the mood is unanimous. Such trips could last "forever."

Kids don't really judge a trip by destination or itinerary but by the adventure and excitement... most of which can be self-created as the scene changes.

It's not *where you are* but *who you're with* that determines the fun and the memories.

* Togetherness is the thing, and there's lots of that when you're together on the water—perhaps on a cruise ship to and from Alaska, or a week on a houseboat on a TVA lake, or even whitewater rafting on Idaho's Salmon River.

  Quietly drifting in the waters of the Everglades, or on the muddy Mississippi, or way up north in the Boundary Waters—each is a magic scene. So too is any flatland lake or farm pond. Boats can be voyager canoes or oil-barrel rafts, just as long as they float most of the time.

  Sailboats—board size, like Sun & Star Fish, or live-aboard, inter-island schooners—open up the world in a child's active imagination.

  Rivers run rampant nationwide, and most have whitewater of various difficulty, but all have quieter water that reaches a seldom seen world accessible only by dirt road or path.

✷ ✷ ✷

Almost every river in the United States of any size, whether flatland or mountainous, hosts outfitters, boat rentals, and guide services. The wilder the water, the more operations there are to thrill young and old, family and friends, church groups and clubs with the joy of whitewater rafting.

Whitewater trips run the gamut from half-day trips to two weeks, and lucky is the extended family that shares the lifetime adventure of a wild-water vacation in country accessible only by river travel.

* The ultimate in family adventure travel just has to be in a chartered sailing yacht. If there's an experienced sailor in the family, bareboat charter is the greatest. But with or without a captain and with or without a cook, there is no greater family fun and freedom. Sail when you like, swim when and where you want, beachcomb at will...and you're hardly ever out of sight or rowing distances from an "exotic island." All the family members mix, mingle, and revel in the experience, from old-timers to teenagers and toddlers.

As travel and lodging costs go, boat charter is not really all that expensive. It's a one-time fee, and your food is as-is and where-is.

* Cities, too, offer true adventure travel—such as Thanksgiving in New York City, with Macy's

* * *

Parade and Radio City, plus all the other big city sights that will serve as reminders and memories for a lifetime.

Any American will be enriched by visiting Washington D.C. for at least a week of walking, gawking, and looking up into domes and down into subway entrances. History current and past is adventure at its greatest, to be relived by kids in every history class and remembered each time they watch the evening news. Pursuing a long-term goal to visit all fifty state capitals is another enrichment builder.

* From South Padre to Cape Cod, and from San Diego to the San Juan Islands, beaches all have that one great thing in common: sand. And so do many creeks, ponds and rivers: sand to build castles in, to "bury" people in, to just lie in and feel the heat of the sun and the cooling of the breeze, to relax in and talk about and wonder where it all came from, how it got there, and how it tames the waves and placates the wind, and lasts and lasts and lasts.

* National and state parks offer a tremendous variety of experiences. Almost every one has hiking trails (or "walking trails," if you prefer the less strenuous-sounding term). All these trails go somewhere (maybe just to the water fountain and restroom, or maybe in and out of the Grand Canyon or Yellowstone's Bear Park), and may tell

* * *

you what you're looking at as you go. There are trails to fit every age, every skill, and every physical condition. Most are free, or at least very, very cheap, if you're old enough to be an NPS Golden Eagle.

To hike a special trail such as Grand Canyon's Bright Angel Trail as a boy, as a father, and then as a grandfather is possible (barely), and is the ultimate test of grandparenting.

* Adventure train trips are as varied as Amtrak's ride from Washington D.C. to Williamsburg, the Durango to Silverton Railroad in Colorado, and the Midnight Sun Express from Fairbanks to Anchorage. Grandchildren love them all, and in many cases it will be their first real train ride.

Who of us will ever forget the sight of dimly lit stations and towns whizzing by, the sound of crossing signals and other trains on passing sidings?

Grandparents remember, as Tex Beneke sang in "Chattanooga Choo Choo," about "dinner in the Diner—nothing can be finer." Eating on some trains means starched tablecloths and multi-choice silver, bringing an opportunity in etiquette training for the youngsters.

The adventure is heightened on longer runs that require sleeping in compartments, berths, or roomettes. Kids are wide-eyed at the miracles

★ ★ ★

that "Pullman Porters" create in turning day into
night.

* Hunting any game bird or animal is never-ending
  pleasure to a hunter, but it is greatly surpassed
  by seeing a son or daughter pass on the skills of
  of hunting to your grandsons or granddaughters.
  Memories of every hunt you and your kids ever
  took come rushing back as wide young eyes thrill
  to the rise of a covey, or a big game stalk.

* "Sleeping out" in a tent or bunk house, preparing
  food over an open fire, talking around the
  campfire, telling stories under the stars, and
  awaking before dawn...all this will etch memories
  that multiply and become more glorious with the
  years.

Is adventure travel expensive? Perhaps. But if a
couple of grandparents decided to travel only half as
much as they could otherwise afford, and yet always
take two or more grandchildren along when they do
strike out, it would more than double their fun. It
would also train those children to someday take
their grandkids along—to see and enjoy the fascinating worlds their grandparents introduced to
them.

* * *

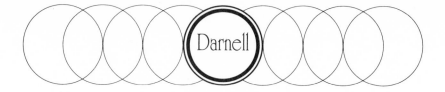

Darnell

TOGETHER TIMES

Y EARS AGO I HEARD Dr. Charles Allen at the First Methodist Church in Houston give another of his superb scriptural sermons, this time on the closing verses in Paul's second letter to Timothy—a poignant and very personal passage in which Paul asked Timothy to bring him writing materials and his coat, and urged him to "come before winter."

Our three sons were at college at the time. Stirred by the portrayal Dr. Allen gave of the impact and power of Paul's letter and his longing to see Timothy, I wrote each son about how important it is for them to stay in regular contact with each other.

That has been my crusade in the family: encouraging everyone to stay in touch, and to get together individually or as families— cousins with cousins, brothers with brothers, sisters-in-law with sisters-in-law...any combination whatever—and to do it whenever and however the opportunity can be made and shared.

It is so sad to see families grow apart and become **almost like strangers. Anything that is worthwhile and meaningful—including family closeness—requires work, but that work makes it all the more precious.**

One of our current family traditions was begun twenty-three years ago when our sons' wives and I started taking an annual trip together. Each year—in a different place each time—it has meant great fun for "the girls": shopping, touring, sunning, reading, playing cards, talking, laughing, playing, sharing.

The men have had great fellowship on trips together as well, just as they used to do as boys with their dad—hunting and camping and canoeing trips, highlighted by sitting and telling stories around a bright, friendly fire. Boys from camp and their fathers often go along as well, and to this day those dads and their sons—now grown and with their own families—will write to Spike and recall the glowing memories they have of those times, and how they want to duplicate them with their grandsons.

Our wedding anniversary at Thanksgiving has been an ideal time for family reunions. Cousins get reacquainted, and everyone benefits from joking and

✿ ✿ ✿

regaling one another, and recalling "the way we were" when we got married (Spike and I take a lot of cajoling on this).

The "Life Rewind Button" gets nearly worn out in these get-togethers, as we "replay" all kinds of wild stories from the past. Everyone—no matter what age—enjoys the time as family jokes are recalled and "too-tall" tales are told on Gran'maw and Pappy. And, of course, more stories are always being recorded on the "Life Rewind" for future call-back.

As our grandchildren grow up they're seeing the merit and worth of frequent togetherness in this family. And when Spike and I aren't around anymore and I can no longer fulfill my self-appointed role to keep the "family torch" fired up and held high, I perceive that our grandgirls Jamie Jo and Courtney will stand in and be the staunch and solid promoters, fanning the flame. Those girls love their cousins, and the feeling is mutual.

One of the best trips I've had lately—short in time but long in memory—was to take part in homecoming weekend at Baylor University, where grandsons Lance and Scott were genuinely pleased I had come to see them at their campus "home away from home." They and their parents invited me, and from the time of arrival to departure it was like Shangri-La in *Lost Horizon*. I couldn't have felt more glamorous and *young* if I had spent the time at the Greenhouse à la Neiman Marcus. What a wholesome and happy atmosphere! I met a stream of attractive,

✿ ✿ ✿

mannerly students, all of them friendly. As Lance exclaimed, "Gran'maw, there are more cool Christians on this campus!" I wanted to head for the Registrar's Office and join up.

Speaking of campuses, I also visited another grandson's campus—Southwest Teachers State University at San Marcos, Texas, where Cody is playing football and studying to become a veterinarian.

I was invited to go in the university's athletic dorm to see Cody's room, and that was "interesting." "Now, Gran'maw," he told me first, "before we go in I want you to know that the posters on the wall are not mine; they're my roommates!" (I'm sure his roommate tells the same thing to his visiting grandmother-in-tennis-shoes.) Actually, the posters were not too shocking—more like the Petty Girls we used to see during World War II—but I wouldn't admit this to Cody; he worried and sweated enough about them.

The visit to Cody's school was wonderful, and I loved being an eyewitness to his world. The students— many from the farms and ranches of West Texas— were friendly there as well. They "howdied" this grandmother all over campus.

Another grandson moved way out West on the Rio Grande River near Mexico—fer, fer away from these Ozark hills, but not too far for Spike to take time

✿ ✿ ✿

and go see Wesley and his mom in their new environs. Spike took a kayak out to Wesley, and they had a fine outing on the Rio Grande.

These trips have further convinced us that we grandparents can stay so much closer through our letters and calls to our older grandkids, once we've seen and experienced their world. Those who share, care!

There are so many ways to make the absences fonder and to keep families from drifting apart. It does require taking the initiative and making the effort, but it's a vital task as far as we are concerned, and grandparents have more time than others in the family to make it happen.

"Blest be the ties that bind..." It's gratifying to see other members now contributing to the binding of family ties. Our sons telephone each other often. Mary Evelyn tells us if her husband Bob gets a late-night call from Bill, Bob chuckles off and on for the rest of the night, recalling their funny conversation (Bill has always been one to "leave 'em laughing").

Our sons' wives have become more like our own daughters. They're "on track" in encouraging family esprit de corps right along with Spike and me.

Family togetherness takes a desire for unity, and plenty of cheerleading.

✿ ✿ ✿

And it's never too late to start, no matter where you are in your family's growth. Just turn on the "Life Rewind Button" whenever you're together, start planning and building traditions of togetherness, be willing to be a cheerleader for the cause...and snugly bind those blessed ties.

✿ ✿ ✿

Spike

PROS NOT
NEEDED

A ROUNDUP OF SPORTS for unlimited enjoyment by grandparent and grand-child alike:

★ One of the lasting legacies of the Kennedy era is family fun on the lawn playing touch football. For a good front-lawn or backyard game of touch football, be it one-on-one or our kids versus your kids, grandkids don't need a Roger Stauback leading Tom Landry's plays. Besides the kids, all it takes is the football (sponge or inflated) and granddad and/or grandma refereeing or passing. Boundaries are vague and flexible, goal lines are "over there" and "back here," and the rules are "no shoving—only two-hand touch."

★ Football season may seem endless but warmer weather eventually arrives—the

★ 115 ★

season for softball and baseball. Lots of kids arrive at Little League not really knowing how to catch a ball because their dad "just didn't have time" and grandpa "lived a long way away." But lucky are the boys and girls who have grand-parents willing to risk sore arms and hurting joints to play "catch" (or bat fungo, or play "pepper"). Playing catch is so easy and handy. Distances start out short for little folks, and get longer as the years go on.

* It was a stroke of sheer genius when Dr. James Naismith hung up that peach basket at ten feet and started the great game of basketball. One-on-one, two-on-two, or just plunking from left field is irresistible and endless fun. The ever-present, never-satisfied challenge presented by a basket, backboard, and ball is simply overwhelm-ing to old and young. The basket is just always up there demanding to be shot into, stuffed, tipped, dunked, or slammed.

In playing with your younger grandkids, the secret is to first hang it at six feet, then eight feet, and only later at ten. If the height of the goal is right, anybody can be a Michael Jordan.

* Dr. Ken Cooper, the aerobics guru, rates rope-skipping at the top as a conditioning exercise, and it's just as high in pleasure—whether there are two hands or four hands swinging the rope, and whether it's "hot pepper" or "over the waves."

* * *

It's "dealer's choice" for grandparents to jump, skip, or swing.

*   The thrill of free-wheeling on a bike is surpassed only by teaching a grandkid to take that first solo ride without the training wheels. Running down the driveway, pushing and balancing and weaving and puffing, is all-fulfilling when finally your kid's little kid takes off alone and shakily looks back, smiles, waves, and rides into the sunset or at least to the next block.

    Great compensation has come now to oldsters in the so-called Mountain Bikes, with their multi-gears, sturdy frames, and almost never flat tires. Now the time we used to spend repairing bikes can be used riding alongside and keeping up, courtesy of mechanical progress.

*   Invention and innovation have also done much to keep older folks in the swim. Fins, snorkel tubes, and dive masks make an all-seeing porpoise out of any recreational swimmer as they relax completely on the surface, kick when desired, and breathe and see at will.

    The great American bathtub is the very place to learn to skin dive (not scuba) or snorkel as you please. A full tub, with or without jacuzzi agitation, can conquer all fears and ease the frustration of "mouth breathing" only, and leave you in a prone position floating and in relaxed comfort.

✱ ✱ ✱

All this is boundlessly rewarded in the big stuff as you flutter-kick alongside a snorkeling grand-kid, pointing out wonders of the deep to each other and sunning your backside at the same time. To add to the enjoyment, one of our grand-sons hums and "kinda sings" as we snorkel along.

* Just like that hanging basketball goal, a ping-pong table—with ball and paddles on the ready —demands action. Grandkids' attention spans are often short and visits are often brief, so things must be READY.

  While playing, grandfolks don't need blistering serves and slant-eyes; they just need to keep the ball in play, and stoop a lot to retrieve errant balls when their handful of them finally runs out.

* Homes fortunate enough to have a pool table become an instant haven for the future Minne-sota Fats or gentlemen eight-ballers. The less shooting ability the grandparent has, the better, so the grandkid feels successful and not over-shadowed. Little ones come on fast with an uncanny and unexplained understanding of angles and ball speeds.

* Backyard badminton, aerial darts (the paddle type), and the new abbreviated tennis-like game of Sport Court can each turn the least of a lawn

* * *

into a juvenile country club. With even mediocre ability (and long arms), you can stand in the middle of the court and do pretty well keeping the bird or ball in play.

* Nowadays most every city or town of any size has a go-cart track. It doesn't take a trip to Disney World to capture the thrill of "drivers education" or Indy 500 racing, with or versus one or more grandkids.

* Even shuffleboard, hopscotch, and jacks are thrilling to kids who haven't worn out their soles and seats already in these pavement sports.

It doesn't take a pro to play and teach a loved child. But remember: Whatever the game, the teacher's ultimate fate is defeat—which is sweeter than victory if the winner is your grandkid, and you "taught him how" and "knew him when."

✷ ✷ ✷

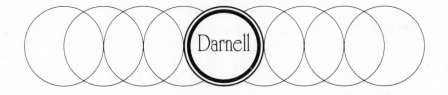
THE MATTER OF MANNERS

P RACTICE GOOD manners, honey," the genteel southern grandmother said to her granddaughter; "Someday they'll come back in style."

Someday they might—with your grandkids and mine leading the way!

Years ago I read of a young person who asked his father, "Why don't we talk together about the day's activities like the families on television do?"

The father declared, "Because those are not real dads...they're Hollywood fruitcakes!"

The boy could only sigh: "But they're always *happy!*"

Being polite is not a weird brand of "Hollywood fruitcake" (especially these days, with what comes out of Hollywood). Being polite and well-mannered means respect and consideration for others—it helps a home be "always happy," and "makes the livin' easy."

Recently, I attended a school program of plays and skits sponsored by a junior high communications class. During the intermission, the home economics students hosted refreshments. An ambiance pervaded the room as we gazed on an intimate setting of small tables with cloths, candles, and cutlery.

As our family was getting seated at our table, Brady, age ten, stood behind my chair to hold it and assist me. I tried to act nonchalant and casually thanked him—as if he had always done this—while silently recalling that a few months earlier I would have wagered against big odds that he'd grow up a yard ape.

Why are we grandparents so surprised when the next generation reflects a little culture and couth? There IS hope!

The practice of good manners begins, of course, at home—in courtesy between father and mother, and between parent and child—as well as in respect and consideration shown to neighbors, sales clerks, grocers, repairmen, and others. Parents and grand-parents must set the example, consistently. How can the kids learn—how can we expect "Please" and "Thank you" from them—if we don't personify

✿ ✿ ✿

respect for each other and to them, as well as to those around us?

Grandparents can take the lead—and get more admiration and loving attention—by being pleasant and gracious around family. We'll be better company that way than if we're full of complaints and commiserations (a sure lead-up to alienation of affections) or if we invade and interfere in our children's lives. With an attractive attitude and good humor, we'll be invited and wanted, not spurned and dreaded.

Spike and I know that our grandchildren see examples of good manners in their parents, and I'm sure they see their grandfather treating their grandmother in the same courteous way. I trust they're learning that to *"Try a Little Tenderness"* gets quite a lot accomplished, and it's enjoyable all the while.

✿ ✿ ✿

Spike

BRIEFING
IT

MILLIONS OF ADVERTISING DOLLARS are spent daily in our mass media to wedge slogans into the minds of young and old—Where's the Beef? Just Say "No." Heartbeat of America. The Real Thing. Have You Driven a _____ Lately? This _____'s for You. (You can fill in the blanks.) And on and on.

The advertisers are taking advantage of something bigger even than their budgets—something we can take advantage of as well: With slogans, titles, and catchwords, great truths and Christian principles can be cut down to kid-size...and thus be remembered, supplying inspiration for a lifetime.

The I'M THIRD message—God is first, others second, and I'm third—is one that automatically brings to mind two of our friends: One of them for eighty-four years lived the I'M THIRD way for all of us to see; the other exemplified

I'M THIRD when he died while guiding his crippled Air Force exhibition jet into a sure-death crash, rather than bailing out and risking the lives of innocent spectators.

The expression I'M THIRD and the stories behind it are something we've found to be priceless gems to remember and pass on. (Some phrases and stories are one-timers, but great ones can and should be repeated over and over again until they become a brain transfusion.) Every kid we've ever contacted has learned how Coach Bill Lantz in his eighty-four years epitomized the exciting, dedicated, inspiring, selfless I'M THIRD life—and that Captain Johnny Ferrier, because he was inspired by Coach Lantz, lived and died an I'M THIRD hero.

As with "I'm Third," here are a few other tags familiar to our family:

* All our kids believe that FOUR SQUARE is the way to grow up and live, because they have heard so many times these words: "Jesus increased in wisdom and stature, and in favor with God and man" (Luke 2:52).

  They know this verse is all the Bible has to say about Jesus' boyhood, and surely that is enough—the "four-square life": wisdom (intellectual maturity), stature (physical maturity), favor with God (spiritual maturity), and favor with man (social maturity).

✶ ✶ ✶

* A ROCK AT A TIME brings instant recall of "Uncle Bob" Calden to the minds of our grand-kids as well as thousands of boy and girl campers, many of whom are grown by now. This man lived almost to be a hundred (he was only a few months short) and he spent so many of those years planting flowers, trees and shrubs to make camp more beautiful. But more memorably, this kindly and educated gentleman—little by little, and by himself—relentlessly built steps down steep trails to make it easier for the campers to climb the hills. A rock at a time, and a bucket of cement at a time, the trails were built.

That's also the way to build a body, a personality, a faith, and a life—it doesn't happen in a flash, but "a rock at a time."

* "AIN'T MISBEHAVIN' " is usually remembered as a song with great lyrics from the Roaring Twenties, but to our granddaughter it means, "I'm saving my love for YOU." And certainly, when she grows up and meets him, she'll realize that saving her love for him was worth it.

* The word CAREFUL expressed to our grand-kids means "eeeasy," "steady in the boat," "quit scrapping," "slow down," or to stop whatever at the moment needs to be stopped. If the use has been long and consistent, a firmly said *"Careful"* can calm the waves of conflict. They get the message, and no fireworks are needed

★ ★ ★

to get it across. (I know it's become effective when the kids begin to mimic my caution: *"CAAARRE-ful!"*

As we adults think back over the tens of thousands of sermons, speeches, lectures, conference messages, seminars, and "discussions" we've heard, it's incredible how little of their content we can actually put our finger on. Much of it has become part of our life one way or another, but remembering it in a form to pass on has escaped us.

Briefing it—sloganizing—puts a handle on those valuable concepts and principles, and makes them easier to recall.

★ ★ ★

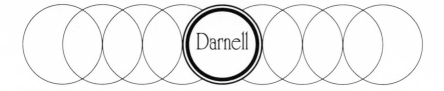

COMING
& GOING

I WAS VISITING in our son Bob's home, and grandson Lance was four years old and just beginning to pray at the table on his own. I had just arrived, and at our first meal together, Lance was called on for the blessing. He prayed, "Thank you for the food and for the hands that prepared it, and let Gran'maw have a safe trip back home." I wondered if that was a clue for me—à la "E.T., go home."

A bit of advice for grandparents is that visits in our children's homes should be short, so our departures are accompanied by genuine remarks of a "Don't-leave-please-stay-longer!" nature. On Pardner's visits to us when Spike and I were a young couple, she used to arrive full of vim and vigor, go through like a Barnum and Bailey circus parade, and then take off. We were left applauding for an encore. Once or twice we even hid her car keys, hoping she wouldn't leave so soon. I now see the wisdom of her method: Better to keep them "glad you're coming" and "sorry you're leaving" than vice versa.

Living close to a son or daughter and their family can be a disadvantage if mannerly considerations against being "too much with us" are not practiced. Since we live close to one son and his family, we try never to telephone them or go visit after the father comes home from work. We respect their family time together, and they as a family deserve their own privacy. Debbie Jo and I can communicate during the day, but "after five" is their time! Occasionally we "drop in" briefly, but only when we've alerted them and checked to see if it's convenient. On the flipside, they treat us to little visits often at our domicile... and they come to see us because they *want* to see us.

"But on the other hand," as Tevye is want to say in *Fiddler on the Roof,* grandparents should also be given the proper courtesy of not being "used" and taken for granted—for example, as babysitters again and again, without due appreciation shown or con- venience considered. I've seen and heard grand- parents who sadly complained that they were not appreciated and thanked.

One year, after a trip into New York City with our young sons, we spent what was our best Christmas ever in colonial Williamsburg. That was a picture- perfect holiday, with all the amenities and traditions of a colonial Christmas—bringing out the Yule Log,

✿ ✿ ✿

a Christmas tree cut and carried from the deep, deep woods, traditional caroling, traditional menus, and of course the decorations everywhere in every home. I'm getting goose-pimples of pride just recalling it now!

On the trip back home to Texas we visited Spike's Uncle Rock and Ankie. Their children and grand-children had just left after having spent the holidays with them, and Uncle Rock and Ankie were a tired twosome. "There's nothing like the patter of little feet —going home!" Uncle Rock declared. When we described the lovely and memorable Christmas in Williamsburg, Uncle Rock excitedly requested Ankie to go to the telephone right there and then and make reservations for a "getaway" Christmas the following year for their family.

Probably all of us at times have shared Uncle Rock's feeling. It's a privilege to have families come back "home," but it can also be wonderful when they go to their own homes again.

✿ ✿ ✿

MEMORY MAKERS

I'VE FORGOTTEN (at age 75, it's easy to do!) when or where I read these words —and I don't think I ever knew *who* said them—but thanks anyway, because they sure are true: **"A good life is determined by the quality of its memories; the moods of a lifetime are often set by the all but forgotten events of childhood."**

As we all know, memories can be good or bad, fun or fearsome, hated or welcome. Fortunately, though, most memories of grandparents seem to be good ones (and I hope that trend continues).

Field and Stream magazine printed the observation that "a sportsman's life must of necessity be filled with months of planning and preparation, moments of realization, and a lifetime of reflection." I believe much the same is true for a grandparent's life.

Maybe an accurate term that describes grand-parents is *"Memory Makers."* What an enviable job description we have!

Recently, in preparation for this writing, I've been asking old and young, "What do you remember about your grandfather or grandmother?" (What an interesting conversation starter that is!) Some of the answers are lurid to ludicrous, but most are happy and healthy. The answers involve faces and places, events and ideas, philosophy and fantasy...and almost always the details are told with a laugh and a smile, and oftentimes a tear.

Memory-making can be a lot of trouble, expensive, and time-consuming, but the rewards—both instant and long-term—are tremendous. The older I get, the more I realize how long memories can last, especially the fun ones. *Doing* is once, but *remembering* is forever. It's fulfilling to know you are part of a mem-orable moment, either as an innocent bystander or as a perpetrator.

Sometimes our exciting (to us) and well-planned (we think) schemes to make memories with our grand-kids don't turn out all that well; but those are the times to regroup and try to out-think these "strange" modern-day youngsters.

The payoff on our memory-making activities may be instant—a profusion of hugs, kisses, smiles, and "thank-you's"—but don't bank on it. Sometimes it can take days, weeks, months or years for kids to

* * *

fully realize how lucky they are to have us for grand-parents.

One thing I'm sure of: We are blessed beyond measure to have grandkids who will share their time and love with us. The benefits to both are immeasurable and everlasting.

★ ★ ★

HOW FIRM
A FOUNDATION

W HEN SEVERAL MEMBERS of the family come to visit, I prepare mounds of food, dishes Spike and I wouldn't normally have (the two of us have settled into a habit of eating disgustingly healthy foods). Knowing that it takes quite a mountain of food to feed the mob, I invariably plan for more than is needed. Whatever leftovers that aren't "toted" away as everyone leaves for home, I freeze to bring out later.

That routine gives me a picture of the way we grandparents can give our love. Do we take the leftover loving and hugging we didn't "serve," store it on ice so it doesn't spoil, and save it for bringing out again at the next opportunity (such as contact by pony express, Ma Bell, or house-calls)? Or are we satisfied with spreading it all out at one sitting?

Do your grandkids see your love as a continual provision, or just an infrequent feast?

It doesn't really take much love for the grandkids to have great memories of their grandparents. Rather, it's the *regularity*, the "always" things we do that are the memory makers.

I once heard a Canadian pastor tell about a humbling lesson on love from his youngest son. It seems the family was poor and had no money to make much-needed repairs on the pastor's car. While alone with the children, the mother conveyed to them the dire need, and asked them to pray for God to see their situation and provide the money. She turned to the youngest boy, who was then three-and-a-half, and said, "You are now a big boy, son; would you pray to the Father to help?"

The boy bowed his head and began his earnest prayer: "Dear Heavenly Father, I know you are always too busy drinking a Pepsi, and can't help us, but..."

The surprised mother was bewildered until she related her son's prayer to her husband. The man shamefully remembered a few times when the boy had pleaded, "Father, would you like to play cars with me?" or "Father, would you come outside with me?"—and the father, with Pepsi in hand, had answered only, "Not now, son, Father's busy—maybe later."

The lesson the pastor learned is for us grandparents as well. We often have busy schedules. But in a grandchild's eyes I wouldn't relish being thought of

✿ ✿ ✿

as being "too busy drinking a Pepsi" that I failed to provide timely love and attention.

When the right love is there, the foundation is there for all that's memorable and best in a grandparent/grandchild relationship.

How firm the foundation...how sweet the memories!

✿ ✿ ✿

ROCK
OF AGES

I T OCCURRED TO ME that the title above would make a noble description of grandparents. I would certainly be proud to be labeled with it. Being a "rock" of a grandparent wraps up a multitude of magic.

It calls to mind a principle that's good not only for parents to be reminded of, but also grandparents: **To survive the winds of the world's whirls, a home must be built of rock on the inside as well as on the outside.**

And what's the rock on the inside? *Love!* Jesus said, "A new command I give you: Love one another. As I have loved you, so you must love one another" (John 13:34).

Once a man talked with a psychiatrist about the best thing he could do for his children. The man had made a list of worthy objectives: providing material necessities, such as food, clothes, shelter, and education; direction and example of religious training; teaching proper social attitudes; and setting good moral standards.

After reviewing the list, the psychiatrist said, "All these are extremely important, but you haven't named the most important thing you can do for your children."

The man wondered aloud what could be more important than the things he had listed, and the psychiatrist replied, "The best thing you can do for your children is to love their mother."

Children need to see LOVE in the home, and it begins when they see the parents exhibiting it, exuding it, executing it.

For us grandparents who are still blessed to have our life-mate at our side, the truth of the psychiatrist's reply can be substantiated as we show love and respect for our spouses.

One of the sweetest chapters about love in the New Testament is the thirteenth chapter of 1 Corinthians. Paul finalizes this eloquent passage by writing, "So faith, hope, love abide, these three; but the greatest of these is love."

We all need love. It is like fresh morning dew on the grass and flowers and trees. We all need nourishing. We need to provide this love potion to our families, our grandchildren, our friends.

✿ ✿ ✿

Giving love has its rewards, but getting it is vital too. Gwynn McLendon Day tells the story of a little girl who sat in her rocking chair hugging and kissing her doll, and speaking words of endearment. As she played with her doll, she also kept glancing across the room to where her mother was working at a desk. Eventually the mother put down her pen, and the child ran to her, climbed on her lap, and said, "I'm so glad you're through—I wanted to love you so much."

"Did you, darling?" the mother asked. "I'm so glad, but I thought you were having a good time with your doll."

"I was, Mommie, but I get tired of loving her because she never loves me back."

Let's be grandparents who know how to "love back" our grandkids. Love 'em in the morning, love 'em in the evening, love 'em all the time—by example, by deeds, by the books we read to them, by the walks we take with them, by the talks we talk with them. *Love 'em.*

Because the Rock of Ages is LOVE... Always has been, always will be!

✿ ✿ ✿

PASS IT ON

H ERE'S A FINE gift idea for a new or soon-coming grandchild: Write a letter to the child in which you tell about the happiness this newcomer brings to you as the latest addition to the family. Write about the joy and anticipation you see in the baby's parents...about the eagerness and excitement with which the child's arrival is surrounded. Write of all the life and love and dreams and aspirations that lie ahead, just for the asking. Write about what the world today is like— today's headline news, the current President of the United States, and the most popular children's TV shows and Disney movies and toys. Cut out and enclose today's comic strips.

But write mostly of your thankfulness for this new grandchild and for all he or she will become to you and to the world.

Won't that be a fine treasure for that grand-child to read and reread years from now, and to someday pass on to your great-grandchildren, and their children too?

Now's the best time to start working on a scrapbook. Include all the snapshots you've accumulated through the years. Poke away at organizing and labeling them. Remember to identify the people in each picture. There may well come a time when no one else will know "who's who" in them except you. (And someday you may forget as well!) Write little descriptions that tell the occasion or setting of the snapshots.

Pass these treasures on! I can promise you that if you don't make them into a "big deal," these price-less things will likely be "tossed" someday. You owe it to the family to spend time documenting such mementos, and no one can do it except you.

Another great idea is to purchase a copy of Bobb Biehl's excellent book entitled *Memories.* Inside are lined pages for you to record just that: your *memories* of all the best things in your life, memories to pass on as a heritage to children and grand-children. You'll find yourself engrossed in the project, and everyone in the family will be grateful and benefited by the loving attention you give to it. (This book can be ordered from Bobb Biehl at P.O. Box 6128, Laguna Niguel, California, 92637.) It makes a worthy and lasting gift to those you love best.

✿ ✿ ✿

I have a file for each grandchild, and in them are stored so many of their letters written over the years, as well such items as the first pictures they drew, cards they sent to me, programs from their various school functions, and so on.

Someday I'm planning to sit back with my feet propped on a footstool in front of a cheerful, chummy fire in the fireplace, and I'll rediscover those messages of love and those art masterpieces... *someday!* And someday...after a grandchild has his own children and will most appreciate these treasures, I will send them to their author and creator.

Weekly letters to your grandchildren don't take a lot of effort. It's a splendid way to keep in contact with the family—and all of us like to go to the mailbox and find personal letters there, don't we?

You don't have to write lengthy epistles (the kids don't have the time and patience to read that much anyway)...just a simple letter addressed with that child's name. You can enclose a riddle...a comic strip that was funny to you in today's paper...a stick of gum...a dollar bill ("go buy an ice-cream cone and think of me!")...a brain-teaser...or perhaps a self-addressed card with questions and fill-in-the-blank questions, to be completed and returned.

My best friend, Sara June, writes letters like Smith-Barney—"the old-fashioned way." She writes with aplomb, providing the most exciting descriptions of

✿ ✿ ✿

all she surveys. All her letters are "keepers," a love-gift cherished by each member of our family. Our sons and daughters-in-love often ask, "Have you heard from Sara June lately? Send us a copy of her latest." She should be syndicated!

It's true we can't all write like Sara June...but **we can *try* harder to make our contact with the family members more pleasurable and impressive.** It can be an opportunity to whet their appetite for "us."

We grandparents are privileged to have such a special possession: *time!* Take time to share your thoughts in writing, to compose amusing stories, and to express love to the family.

Many of us also have access to something that grandparents never had before: computers! My new office computer has opened new windows of freedom for me to write longer, newsier letters...the same to each son's family! If I want to "single out" anyone, I can add notes with individual messages at the end.

Another family fun idea: Draft a questionnaire for the grandchildren to answer about their parents. Make up questions (you can vary the difficulty of them according to the children's ages) and leave blanks to be filled in. This can be a sneaky way to get them to ask you questions about what you know best—and to help them learn more about their parents and you as well. You'll likely be surprised at how little of this knowledge your grandkids are

✿ ✿ ✿

aware of. (We've played this game and are amazed how a family can be so close and in daily communication, and still know so little about one another.)

Here are sample questions:

1. *What was your mother's maiden name?*
2. *What is your father's middle name?*
3. *Where was your mother born?*
4. *Where was your father born?*
5. *What schools did your mother attend?*
6. *What schools did your father attend?*
7. *What jobs have your father and mother held since leaving school?*
8. *Where do your parents work now? If they have bosses, what are their names?*
9. *Where did your father first meet your mother?*
10. *What is the date of their wedding anniversary?*
11. *Where were they married?*
12. *Did they go on a honeymoon? If so, where?*

The questions that could be asked are endless—and the results will be amusing for everyone, besides providing a great opportunity for the grandchildren to learn more about their heritage.

Roots are agents for nourishment and stability, and knowing more about them is a pleasure—everyone likes to *belong*. Helping grandkids learn more about their roots is a task for which grandparents are the best equipped...so "have at it"—and make it fun.

✿ ✿ ✿

WAVING THE FLAG

AS PRESIDENT REAGAN remarked in his farewell address, the family dining room table is the best place to teach patriotism. Mealtime is certainly a handy time for us "veterans" to tell war stories and to "spread tradition," both family and national.

Beyond the dining room, visiting the places where history happened (and is happening) is also a prime teaching tool, as well as great family fun. With videos, slides, and storybooks to reinforce the impact, it can all be brought alive in minds young and old.

There is much more to patriotism than remembering wars and battles, but to the young, nothing beats seeing the two-hundred-year-old earthworks at Yorktown, the rolling hills of Gettysburg, the trenches at Vicksburg, the reconstructed forts on the Great Plains, the Alamo in Texas, and the sweep of the Little Big Horn. The young 'uns who visit these can "smell the powder burning," they can see the flag waving "by dawn's early light," and hear the shouts and bugles and guns.

As children's minds expand, patriotism can be broadened into non-violent adventures: trips to NASA at Cape Canaveral and Houston, TVA dams and atomic power plants, GM and Ford factories, New York City's skyline, San Francisco's bridges, Mount Rushmore, and yes, even Disney World and Disneyland, which have become world-renowned images of the American spirit.

Plymouth Rock, Jamestown, Old Ironsides, Connecticut's Mystic Seaport of whaling days, the vast citrus groves of Florida and the Southwest, the rolling Mississippi from Minnesota to New Orleans, the endless corn and wheat fields of the Middle West, and the "purple mountain majesties" beyond—these teach patriotism awesomely, imparting the vastness and might of our beloved country.

Parades, picnics, theme-park visits and sports games can all be "flag-wavers" as well, and the same is true for family discussions of current national and world events.

"Showing the flag"—the bigger the better, at home and abroad, in peace and in war—can be a growing experience, and who better to bring it about than grandparents who, in the eyes of their grandkids anyway, "saw it all happen"—and who perhaps have traveled enough and seen enough to learn that America is the best of all homes.

✶ ✶ ✶

READING

G RANDSON CODY often returned to spend more time with us while his younger brother Wesley underwent further treatment for diabetes. It was during the time that our country's bicentennial was being celebrated, and Cody and I read every Landmark book we could find on the Revolutionary War, the Constitution, John Paul Jones and his adventures at sea, George Washington, Benjamin Franklin, Paul Revere and more. I had as much enjoyment and education from all that reading as Cody did—and I also benefitted because I influenced it and shared it. Cody became an enthusiastic and eager reader, reading all the books the library had to offer his inquisitive, sponge-like mind.

Jamie Jo often brings her library books to me, saying, "Gran'maw, you'll just love this book. I can keep it out for a few more days if you want to read it." I do, and then we discuss it.

It has been a tradition with Joe and Debbie Jo's family that Gran'maw takes each child to sign up for his first library card at our local library when he reaches his sixth birthday. Having this card is a major privilege, one each child feels pride in attaining. He goes to the librarian, Mrs. Norma Root, and announces, "I'm old enough now to get my own card." Mrs. Root treats him as an adult, and goes through the proper routine: "Welcome to the Taneyhills Community Library! Will you please sign this card and write your name, address, and phone number on it?"

These children make the same discovery I have: The library is a wonderful world! Visits there have the rosiest effect on my day. The lady volunteers who work there are always as friendly and lovely as the books that surround them. If I were not employed, I think I would want to join them and help at the library. I'd be wrapped in a blanket of bliss.

On the first warm days of summer, I often invite a grandchild to bring a book and go lie on a quilt under a big shady tree, to prop against the trunk...and read!

When I was a young girl, I enjoyed reading more than anything else in the world. And when at the library, as I looked over books trying to decide which ones to check out, I remember I always looked at the last page to see if "they lived happily ever after."

✿ ✿ ✿

I still want everyone to live happily ever after. And I know I can be influential in aiding our grand-children to achieve that goal as I encourage them to read.

✿ ✿ ✿

NEW KID
ON THE BLOCK

B randi looked at me with her Precious
Moments eyes, and announced,
"Gran'mawwhite (all one word), you
rock-and-roll my heart."

Let me tell you, this little ol' tennis-shoed
grandmother has been honored with some
scrapbook-keeper, heart-and-soul heavies from
ever-lovin' grandchildren, but this one from
Brandi was stuff to save and savor.

Brandi is our "new kid on the block." She is a
step-grandchild whom we GET to love and
cherish along with the others, who "go back a
long way." (God is so good—He gives us big
hearts that read "Open for Business; Please
Enter!")

Brandi is a precocious (I can say that without
bragging because she doesn't have any "White"
genes to mess her up) four-year-old who falls
in the same category as so many thousands of

other children of divorced parents. She has "extra" grandparents, and that can be and should be to her advantage if we do our part by reinforcing the fact that she is loved by each grandparent (and, yes, by each parent and step-parent), and that she is fortunate to have so MANY who love her. I encourage Brandi to tell us about the other grandparents and the good times she has when visiting them.

Most children—and not just the ones from broken homes—aren't listened to enough, or given enough opportunities to talk about their daily experiences, and the changes that enter their lives. Grandparents can help! When we listen to them, it builds a rapport that is vital for sturdy relationships.

Teach your grandchildren to think positively. You can make a game of it by building approaches to bright and happy conversations. Pretend "tea parties" and similar "playing-like" games are a natural way to do this, and to cultivate closeness. It's surely one of the most pleasant of child games I know. It has lots of points to commend it for: It stirs the child's (and yours too) imagination and creative juices; it easily breaks conversational barriers and helps the child relax if he or she is shy and reticent; and it brings out openness. These "tea parties" later grow easily and naturally into tête-à-tête sit-down visits over a cup of cocoa when the child has outgrown "tea parties."

One of the most outstanding social events for me was a "high" tea I gave for granddaughters Jamie Jo and Courtney and several of their friends. Their

✿ ✿ ✿

Cabbage Patch dolls were also invited. The girls came dressed in their best "bib and tucker," and pleasantries were exchanged as we had tea, with our little "pinkies" much in evidence. The dolls had a special place set up for them, and the "ladies" would go to their "children" to tend to their needs. Later in the afternoon there were a few parlor games with pens and pads. Occasionally, even now one of these girls will ask me, "When are we going to have another party with our Cabbage Patch dolls?

Good communication with boys can be reinforced and renewed in different ways—a walk through the woods, shooting BB guns at tin can targets set on posts, playing catch, training pups, sailing boats, playing in a sandpile—all these are good.

I find it disturbing and heart-breaking that we adults aren't sensitive enough and compassionate enough to realize that our ugly words and feelings and reactions are thoughtlessly and selfishly thrust into a child's heart. Sometimes that deposit of ugliness abscesses, and there is no escaping its pain. How *dare* we do this!

Maybe grandparents can ease that pain and release the stress and hurt. There are ways to do it, and you and I are needed for the job.

The best thing we can do for grandchildren, be they "yours," "theirs" "ours" or whose ever, is to **never, never say anything derogatory and degrading about any of the parents.** This brings only hurt—

✿ ✿ ✿

to the children, to the parents, and to everyone. It definitely hurts you, tarnishing your image with one and all.

True communication with our grandchildren (or with anyone) is a reward given only for excellence in effort. It can't be had by bribery or bartering. It's a distinct and individual attainment that must be earned.

✿ ✿ ✿

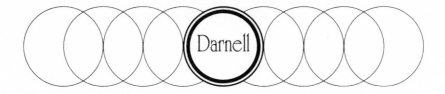

METHODIST PALLETS

M Y IRISH GRANDMOTHER probably invented the "Open Arms Policy." There were always from ten to fourteen children living in her home. The older boys often brought in stray children they had met up with, and since there was food to share on their East Texas farm and adequate help to work it, Grandmother "took 'em in" and made them feel at home. (While growing up having so many uncles and aunts, I didn't realize that many of them were not my "blood" kin.)

For transportation, a big wagon was always available to pile in all the kids and cousins. Everyone was included in trips to town or church.

For sleeping, having a new orphan or homeless child was no consequence either—it only meant "move over" in bed, or else quilts and pillows were put down in a big pallet for on-the-floor sleeping—the closer the cozier. They called it a "Methodist pallet," but I never found out why it wasn't labeled some other denomination (my own grandparents were Baptists, and my great-grandfather was a Baptist minister.)

These old-fashioned home-and-family, the-more-the-better values carried over as strong reference points in the home I grew up in. We always had a mess of company, and the livin' was easy and enjoyable. My mother, a single parent who's been by herself most of her life, always encouraged my friends to come to our house for fun and games. Our house was a favorite hangout (she knew we had to go somewhere, and home was the best place).

I wish we had kept a Methodist Pallet Guest Book in my high school years when many kids came over on weekends to spend the night with us—sometimes boys *and* girls. Mother would be in the middle on the floor with us, talking, tittering, and telling tales most of the night. My friends' parents were content to know Mother was there as chaperone.

All this was during the depression days when you made your own fun. Life was rugged and ragged, but we didn't know it.

Spike and I have used the Methodist Pallet Party Plan while raising our boys, too, and it's still a prac-tice here. It's the easiest and most fun way to have grandchildren drop in and stay for a night or two, and provides a festive atmosphere. Best of all, there are not a lot of beds for me to clean up and make afterwards (that alone is reason enough to try it).

✿ ✿ ✿

Sometimes I invite all the children at once, but usually just boys or just girls, and sometimes just one at a time with several of his or her friends.

Sometimes, when just the grandchildren come, I spread out the pallet on the living room floor, and I bed down on the couch beside them. We laugh and talk until Morpheus sets in. Then I cut out, and go crawl into the comfort of our bed with Spike for the rest of the night. Of course, there is usually at least one grandkid who awakens later on and comes climbing into the big cozy bed with us. By daylight I might even end up on the floor by myself—but that's the state of the art. I can always catch up on a good uninterrupted night of sleep during the long dry spells when they're not with us.

If they've been busy with school and the extracurricular activities that seem to engulf them, and we haven't had the pleasure of their company in a while, we *make* ways to entice them to come. Not only does it fill the need for us to be with them and for them to be with us, but they enjoy the change of atmosphere from their home to ours, and it's something special they can share with their friends. It's been a good way to share in their lives and stay on a communicative plateau with each one.

We've found that a sleeping bag is a wonderful choice for a grandchild's Christmas or birthday present. They can be used for slumber parties during the school year and at camp in the summer, and they can bring them to our house when they come to spend the night.

❀ ❀ ❀

Setting up a tent in the back yard on a summer evening is an event for everyone. The younger ones may decide to go in the house around midnight if you aren't with them, but the daring adventure is well worth the experience of being scared by what-ever's "out there." I've often slept in the tent with them, and I, too, could hear all kinds of weird noises that made me think how much I wanted to be in my own safe, snug bed.

If you're a new grandparent, you're fortunate to have all these experiences ahead of you. It reminds me of the story of the ten-year-old boy Tom who was watching his newborn baby brother, Robert. Tom told his mother, "Robert is sure lucky!"

"Why do you think so?" his mother asked.

"Because he gets to do all them new things... learning to climb trees, and to feel the wind on his face when he runs, and to wade in the creeks, and to roll on the grass, and to hold a new pup—you know, all them new things!"

You new grandparents are lucky too—you get to do "all them new things," things that we have learned to cherish.

Enjoy them all! And don't forget the Methodist pallet.

✿ ✿ ✿

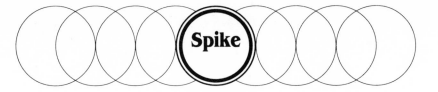

EVALUATION

EVERY DAY in the media, coaches and players in professional and collegiate sports are evaluated. What a come-uppance it would be if teachers, preachers, parents—and yes, grandparents—were evaluated just as frequently, as publicly, and as effectively.

Come to think of it, preachers' results are never fully evaluated until Eternity, and maybe that's the way it is with grandparents as well. Nevertheless, it would be enjoyable (maybe) and certainly beneficial if our grandparenting could be evaluated before it's too late. How nice not to have to wait for our eulogy to find out "how we did."

Recently our grandkids, at the urging of their parents, taped their memories and impressions of their grandparents. The full range of them, from preschoolers to college students—in their own unique way, in private, and at their own speed—tape-recorded their comments—"I remember when Gran'maw and Pappy..." etcetera.

Later—much later—upon hearing it all, Darnell and I were amazed and amused at all they did remember, and, frankly, at all they forgot, or at least did not mention during that go-round. (Our publisher has selected many of these comments and included them in the back of this book; so now their evaluation of mine and Darnell's performance is "open to the public.")

For many of us, opportunities for being with and around our grandchildren may be fleeting and few and far between. We "may never pass this way again." We can be so glad we did what we did when we did—while at the same time wishing we'd done more.

One thing is certain: **We *will* be evaluated.**

Just like always, Christ said it best: He set the time-table for our grandparental ministry (and for all our ministry) as better too soon than too late. Remember that "certain rich man" who, being tormented in hell, begged for a messenger to be sent to his five brothers to warn them of their earthly errors before it was "too late"? Sadly enough, it was already too late.

Be encouraged by the example of all those grandparents who made their grandparenting count while it could, and whose influence lives on after them. We

✴ ✴ ✴

recently received a letter from the number four grandson of the late Senator Stuart Symington. The young man commented on the memorial service for his grandfather in Washington's National Cathedral, a service at which four inspiring eulogies were given. The grandson said these eulogies "served me like a great coach in the half-time talk of the biggest game. *It was exciting and positive—just like my Grandpa.*"

✶ ✶ ✶

TO BE OR
NOT TO BE

WHEN OUR son Bob's wife, Mary Evelyn, was president of the Woman's Club in Bryan, Texas, she wrote to us about a certain meaningful talk presented to the ladies of the club. The speaker gave a list of twelve "Be's" to live by. They cover the gamut, and I think they are especially worthy to pass on to all grandparents (and potential grandparents) of all ages, male or female:

1. *Be there*
2. *Be prepared*
3. *Be a hugger*
4. *Be caring*
5. *Be yourself*
6. *Be motivated*
7. *Be professional*
8. *Be positive*
9. *Be a good influence*
10. *Be enthusiastic*
11. *Be kind to everyone*
12. *Be a Believer*

In a nutshell, aren't these what we all should be? If we would "be" these things, we would "be" leaving this world a better place than we found it. And don't you desire that as much as I do?

Some of these "Be's" stir further thoughts…

That first one, BE THERE, just has to be a biggie! There's a need more and more for grandparents to help fill a prize niche kids have: their need for a close-at-hand adult friend. Kids and parents are so caught up with the competitive, commercial curriculum of today's society—at home, at school, at play, at every turn of the day—that there just has to be someone "out there" that *is* there! Letting our grandchildren (and children) know we're "there" when they need us gives them the comfort and security they deserve.

BEING PREPARED would have to include staying in contact and being a part of the younger and youngest generations, not necessarily approving of any lowered standards, but being informed and understanding in order to have wise counsel and "input" when asked. Being prepared versus not being prepared is like the difference between reading *Time* magazine every week, and saving up all fifty-two issues to read once a year—it's so much harder to "catch up" on happenings than it is to "stay up" with them.

✿ ✿ ✿

BE A HUGGER! Isn't that the easiest "Be"? Last summer a generous friend of Joe's gave us a new black Labrador puppy to replace our good Lab dog that died. The puppy was delivered during the final ceremonies of a closing session of camp (attended by the campers' parents), and Joe used the puppy in a family vespers talk. He held the puppy and mentioned to the parents of the teenage campers how "EVERYBODY LOVES 'EM WHEN THEY'RE PUPPIES"—the point being that our kids who are so lovable when they're in the backyard swing set (still "puppies") grow up into adolescents who may not seem so charming to us. But teenagers do need lots of hugs from us every chance we get.

And that's more the reason for us to write our letters and keep communications active when we aren't close at hand to give "honey in the morning, honey in the evening, honey at suppertime." Even if we can't "hug" them physically as often as we would like, you and I can always write to them of our feelings of love and pride for each one, and we can try to convey our confidence in their worthiness. There *are* ways to show it!

BE CARING! Remember the lovely song, "Do You Really Care?" That title says it all. And you *will* really care as you realize how grandparents are needed in so many ways. Learn those needs, and show your care and concern by giving your very best to meet them.

✿ ✿ ✿

BE YOURSELF! Doubtless there are many ways of interpreting "Be yourself" —and this is another one:

Each of us, of course, is changing—sometimes those changes make for improvement as we get older, but sometimes we become like an irregular conjugation: better, badder, bitter. It's so easy to get into a tired old rut and lose spontaneity and spunk and become just another worn-out, wrung-out person.

Remember when you were "FUN"? And maybe witty and clever? When you weren't so jaded and removed from the effervescence of a new day dawning? Decide now to recapture those times. We would all be better company for each other (and ourselves) if we would relax and rediscover a youthful outlook on life. Let's "green up" our growth. Be alive!

Are we retiring into the life of comfort and leisure too much to BE MOTIVATED? Rather than getting moti- vated, it's easier, I agree, to settle in that recliner to watch the evening news and read our library books, occasionally looking across the room and maybe exchanging a little talk with our spouses, or perhaps just sitting there and counting the newest moles and visible veins that have developed. It's easier—but not "funner," and definitely not healthier. Making excuses to "stay in" and "stay put" sets up atrophy of the heart.

Let's take up the challenge and get motivated! Grandkids will be amazed when we do, and we'll probably amaze ourselves! Years can be dropped

✿ ✿ ✿

from our weary, wrinkled countenances, to be replaced with brighter eyes and smiling faces.

Try taking up dancing together! The best dancers I've seen—and the couples having the most fun— are the AARP folks, couples over 60, 70, and even 80! Last summer two granddaughters joined us on a cruise-tour of Alaska, and the girls were wide-eyed with admiration for the "grandparent types" who could dance so professionally. They didn't laugh at Spike and me either when we took to the floor, but beamed with pleasure!

Staying romantic and being fun together will help keep us motivated and energetic—and makes us more attractive to our loved ones and to others. Be inspirational! Be scintillating!

BEING A GOOD INFLUENCE is one of the best ways I know to be a good grandparent. We've all developed and taken on habits that certainly aren't always commendable or on the Good Conduct List, and these things won't be a good influence on our grand-children. We may contend that what we do to our-selves and our own health is "our own business"— but is it really? Certainly not when a grandchild's eye is watching (and they see far more than we think).

Being a good influence also includes supporting our grandchildren's parents in their "rules for rearing." Everything we say and do with and for the grand-children must be "parent-approved." Double stan-

✿ ✿ ✿

dards (theirs versus ours) do not show loyalty, and only hurt the grandchildren as well as the parents. Over the long haul, it will also damage and demean our own character in everyone's eyes. Yes, in our dealings with grandkids, we need the "stamp of approval" from their parents.

Which reminds me of a day long ago when our son Bill was about six years old. His buddy David called and asked if Bill could come out and play. I told David that Bill had gone to the picture show with his brothers. David was disappointed, and asked, "Mrs. White, do you know if that movie was approved by *Parent's Magazine?*"

BE ENTHUSIASTIC! We can all use more enthusiasm. As the big and small events of life come our way, learning to be excited about what might otherwise be considered mundane will be like the Fountain of Youth discovered.

In her book *And So It Goes*, television personality Linda Ellerby quotes a letter from a young girl:

> "Dear Miss Ellerby: When I grow up, I want to do exactly what you do. Please do it better."

That letter is loaded, isn't it? Hits hard!

Enthusiasm is the best "Rx" for better living that I know. Show your grandchildren you can match them in being "charged up" for life.

✿ ✿ ✿

BE KIND TO EVERYONE—Like all habits, habits of kindness are formed a little at a time. So is the habit of *failing* to be kind. It's so easy to get slovenly and sloppy in our relationships with loved ones and everyday companions; and these failures in courtesy set a pattern that others (including grandkids) pick up and follow all too readily. "Monkey see, monkey do" and "Charity begins at home" are old adages (guess it takes one to know one)—but they're applicable here.

The most important "Be" of all is the last one, and it rates a "10"—BE A BELIEVER! Of course my first thought here is of believing in our Lord and Savior. You could also say we need to believe in the individual worth of all men and women and in the future of the younger generation, and you could add a basic trust in our fellow man and patriotic loyalty to country—again, setting an example for our children's children. All the above, however, can be accomplished if we are truly believers in the Lord   s and ask for His divine help and guidance.

✿ ✿ ✿

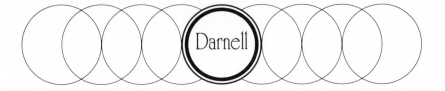

Darnell

GOING ON

ECAUSE OF THEIR devotion and dedication to parenthood, I have the greatest admiration for most young couples I see, as well as our own children with their families. Many of these mothers get more accomplished and do a better job raising their kids than seems possible. They are organized, and seem to be relaxed and enjoying every minute of their harried and busy schedules. They are exercising, serving the community, attending Bible studies, teaching, running a happy home with well-adjusted children, and enjoying good times with their husbands. Many of them are also holding down responsible positions in the working world, yet managing their households at the same time.

The end results will be seen in whether it all works out as well as or better than the way it did when young mothers in my generation stayed home all day.

Of course, not all mothers fit the total picture described above, especially when it comes to the happiness of their marriages. There have been many more divorces, resulting in single mothers raising families and having to make the living.

The scene has certainly changed, along with many values and ideals.

I watched Frank Capra's classic movie *It's A Wonderful Life* for the eighth or ninth time recently, and had the nostalgic feeling of "how it was" when neighbors and friends kept the true meaning of Christmas in their hearts. Real love and concern and compassion for one another was evidenced.

I read that Frank Capra was once asked if there was still a way to make movies like *It's a Wonderful Life*. Mr. Capra answered, "Well, if there isn't, we might as well give up."

That's another reason why our role as grandparents is so important: **We have to keep encouraging the younger generation to hold fast to the high standards and values we have instilled, and not to give in.**

I observe fathers today setting aside special times for family togetherness. They are so pressured, it seems, to provide for their families that they are kept away from home many nights, just to make a living. This interrupts the important routine of family life together. And it means moms are in

✿ ✿ ✿

demand all the more to do the job of parenting for both of them. It is tough on everyone!
Once these mothers and fathers have raised their children successfully under such trying situations, they deserve diplomas as *summa cum laude* graduates of the school of parenting.

Then all they've learned—the paradigm of principles and plans for good marriages and families—will be the prerequisites for their task as grandparents.

It will, of course, be slightly—if not drastically—different from parenting. An appropriate word from Scripture for them would be Joshua 3:4—"You have not passed this way before."

And yet, if all those years gone by were filled with learning to care and encourage and love and live, the lessons will all come back to guide them once more.

Robert Fulgham's fine and witty writing in *The Kansas City Times* a long while back suggests that we were getting prepared as long ago as kindergarten days for the life situations we find ourselves in today. The piece below offers a valuable perspective for grandparenting.

Most of what I really need to know about how to live and do and how to be...I learned in kindergarten! Wisdom was not at the top of the graduate school mountain, but there in the sandbox at nursery school.

✿ ✿ ✿

These are the things I learned: Share everything. Play fair. Don't hit people. Put things back
where you found them. Clean up your own mess.
Don't take things that aren't yours. Say you're sorry
when you hurt somebody. Wash your hands before
you eat. Flush! Warm cookies and cold milk are
good for you. Live a balanced life. Learn some and
think some and draw and paint and sing and dance
and play and work every day—some! Take a nap
every afternoon. When you go out into the world,
watch for traffic, hold hands, and stick together.

Be aware of wonder. Remember the little seed in
the plastic cup: The roots go down and the plant
goes up, and nobody really knows how or why, but
we are all like that. Goldfish and hamsters and
white mice and even the little seed in the plastic
cup...they all die. So do we.

And then remember the book about DICK AND
JANE and the first word you learned, the biggest
word of all: LOOK.

Everything you need to know is in there somewhere. The GOLDEN RULE and LOVE and basic
sanitation. Ecology and politics and sane living.
Think of what a better world it would be if we all,
the whole world, had cookies and milk about 3:00
o'clock every afternoon, and then lay down with our
blankets for a nap...OR...if we had a basic policy in
our nation and other nations always to put things
back where we found them and clean up our own
messes.

And it is still true, no matter how old you are,
when you go out into the world, it is best to hold
hands and stick together.

✿ ✿ ✿

After reading that fine writing again, I feel I must be in my second childhood. I could stand up and put my right hand over my heart and declare all the above as MY CREED.

✿ ✿ ✿

OUR SECOND CHANCE

A WHILE BACK, two motivated, energetic, and "with it" young attorneys visited us in our home. One, a young woman, asked me, "What is your goal for the rest of your life?" (The question wouldn't surprise me if it were directed to one of our sons or their wives, or anyone their age. But a grandmother in her seventies?)

I answered, "I've never had *goals*—or at least I haven't applied that word to any plans or any directions I want my life to take. I don't suppose I have ever had but one desire in my married life of fifty-two years except to be a good wife to Spike—the best I can be—and a good mother and a good mother-in-law...and now also to be a godly woman for the family and the grandchildren to see."

It is just that simple. And I've been blessed to be able to fill that niche. I keep trying and reaching to complete that purpose.

The unexpected ecstasies and joys that have happened have only made it more thrilling along the way. **Nothing good that happens to us is ever lost in our life**; it just becomes a part of our character.

While raising me, my mother gave me the greatest of gifts: the example of her independence, her good humor, her service to her neighbors, her love for flowers, her appreciation for food and shelter. She helped me learn as a little girl to get up early, and be excited for the day and its gifts. Anne in *Anne of Green Gables* said it best: "This day has never happened before; there are no mistakes in it!"

I have tried to pass this *joie de vivre* on to our grandchildren. Jamie Jo used to stay with us for a week or two at a time when her parents were traveling to promote our camp programs (this was before Joe and Debbie Jo added other children and then a housekeeper to stay with all of them).

Awakening Jamie Jo in the early morning I would sing softly, "Lazy Mary, will you get up, will you get up...so early in the morning?...If you get up, I'll give you: a golden egg, a beautiful prince, or a diamond ring...Which will you chose?" She would play right along and act sleepy and say, "None of them." Then I'd start the song again mentioning other ridiculous choices. It was just a game, but a nice warm way to awaken.

Even when grandchildren are very young, walking

✿ ✿ ✿

outside with them and talking about the trees and the wind, or looking at night at the moon and the stars, has a lasting effect on their awareness and appreciation of the wonders in their world. (Rachel Carson's *The Silent Spring* is a marvelous guide for just this development.)

I was a grandmother before I really learned the names of many wildflowers and the derivation of their names, their stories and meanings, and now I take close-up photographs of these flowers as well. Learning about them enriches me, an enrichment that is shared with the grandchildren. Along with them I am learning and living in the caress of life.

> To see a world in a Grain of Sand
> And a Heaven in a Wild flower,
> Hold Infinity in the palm of your hand
> And Eternity in an hour.
> —*William Blake*

The children know my interests, and they are always bringing me treasures to be placed on the sill over our kitchen sink: little bouquets of flowers, discarded birdnests, first-colored fall leaves, newborn leaves of spring, and "friendship" rocks (the kind that have little holes in them, and can be strung on a leather thong or cord and worn around the neck.) These all help me "to kiss the joy as it flies..."

Outside our kitchen in front of the breakfast table are two feeders for birds, a watering trough for them (and for the squirrels), and a suet feeder for the woodpeckers. We all enjoy watching the show

✿ ✿ ✿

outside, and the children have learned the names of the birds.

Being a grandparent is like having a second chance in life. Along with our grandchildren, we can be young all over again.

"While we have youth in our hearts," Oliver Wendell Holmes wrote, "we can never grow old." Besides the self-satisfaction and pleasure such a youthful heart brings to us, it also spreads to others in the family. Being interested in all things lends a childlike sense of anticipation that's contagious.

James H. S. Bossard wrote, "Good family life is never an accident but always an achievement by those who share it." As a step toward that achievement, let us strive to keep an active and open mind that is ready each morning to find something new and thrilling in whatever the day brings.

✿ ✿ ✿

LOOKING UP

O N SEEING that fresh glow in the eastern sky: "Wake up, Gran'maw; God has started the world again!"

Such a pre-game bonfire may be more exciting to a young one than the game itself is to an old grad.

When on a group outdoor excursion, I was photographing a beautiful auburn-haired yuppie backlit by a Scottish sunrise. I was startled when she admitted this was the first sunrise she had ever seen. I calculated that in her thirtyish years she had missed 11,000 or more sunrises. What a waste!

Holiday Inn's slogan is "The best surprise is no surprise." It's a great phrase for complacent, comfort-loving oldies, but for youngsters the best surprise is the biggest surprise. And it happens every day.

There's usually no family competition for a grand-kid's time at daybreak, and if plans are made the night before, the young one will probably be wide awake and sitting on ready.

Predawn is a magic time because the last chill of night mixes with anticipation and wonder: *What will the sunrise be like today?*

Night birds and nocturnal animals are getting in their last licks at finding breakfast (or supper), and the daylight-loving feathered and furred friends are already up and moving, each in his own way.

Outdoors at dawn, there is never a dull moment.

Then comes the big show as inch by inch the blazing ball rolls up into view. Things rev up everywhere, and the "world starts again."

On cloudy mornings the glimpse of the sun may be brief, but this is special too, because "We caught its only appearance all day."

Such times beget a shared sensation of the birth of time, and provide the right atmosphere for warm little chats about all that can happen today, in our world and everyone else's.

Sunset times together just seem to happen, but these can be planned too—from mountaintop, lakeshore, sea coast, or living-room window.

★ ★ ★

Brilliant, ever-changing colors embellished with vapor trails and man-made dust and smog are always kaleidoscopic, and are never repeated in just the same way.

Moonrise, especially when full, is a silence-producer and a memory-maker for young and old. The mystery and magnificence of a full moon, whose appearance is so predictable, is a scheduled reminder of God's timetable for everything.

Opportunities are endless for family-shared star study—with just two or the whole gang "lying out" on the grass. With a strong-beam flashlight pointing out planets and constellations, seeing and naming them opens up Greek and Roman mythology as well as Bible truths. Understandably, God's greatness takes on a breathless dimension of immensity as little ears hear older mouths talk of galaxies, meteors, and lots more in the heavens.

"Yes," someone said, looking up, "there must be plenty of room in heaven for all of us...wherever it is."

✴ ✴ ✴

*HAVE
FUN!*

SCRAPBOOK

■ PART ONE ■

Our Votes for Quotes

■

Activities

■

Memories

OUR VOTES FOR QUOTES

> *At age 75*
> *Marion Anderson said,*
> "If you've had an active life,
> you don't have to prove it
> to anyone."

> The Measure of a Life,
> after all, is not its
> duration but its
> donation. How much
> will you be missed?"
>
> — *Peter Marshall*

> Each day you can figure,
> "I have not passed this way before...
> and I will not pass this way again."
> Today is unique. Don't let its wonderful moments
> go by unnoticed and unused.

> *From*
> *CLOWNS OF GOD*
> *by Morris West:*
>
> "Keep your mind open
> so that the light can
> always come in;
> Keep your heart open
> so that Love will never
> be shut out."

> How many of us
> in LIFE can say,
> "I have made a difference"?

> **Good old days
> start with good new
> days like today.**

> *Over doors at the Library of Congress*
> *in Washington, D.C.:*
>
> THE PAST IS PROLONGED

OUR VOTES FOR QUOTES

TROPHIES
are important
only if you have
someone to
share them
with.

*—from
PASSAGES*

SOMETIMES

Across the fields of yesterday
He sometimes comes to me,
A little lad just back from play —
The lad I used to be.
And yet he smiles so wistfully
Once he has crept within,
I wonder if he hopes to see
The man I might have been.

—Thomas S. Jones, Jr.

A man who has had good parents
is TWICE blessed:
first when they were alive,
and second, for the memory of them.

Perhaps
the
measure
of LIFE
is not its
length
but its
LOVE.

I have endeavored
to do all the good I
could with the
talents committed
to me, and to honor
God with my sub-
stance.

*—Rev. William
Smith, the father
of Abigail Adams
(Mrs. John Adams)*

FAMILY COURT

One would be in less danger
From the wiles of the stranger
If one's own kin and kith
Were more fun to be with.

—Ogden Nash

TIME'S PACES

When as a child I laughed and wept,
TIME crept.
When as a youth I waxed more bold,
TIME strolled.
When I became a full-grown man,
TIME ran.
When older still I daily grew,
TIME flew.
Soon I shall find, in passing on,
TIME gone.

—Canon Henry Twells
(1823-1900); lines appearing
on an old clock in Chester Cathedral
in England

Seeds
scattered on
the wind
germinate in
their own time.

"How will we
know who we
are without
our past?"

—from THE
GRAPES OF
WRATH
by John
Steinbeck

One must wait until the evening
to see how splendid the day was;
one cannot judge life until death.

— Sophocles

The cistern
contains,
the fountain
overflows.

— William Blake

Oh, it's a long, long while
from May to December,
but the days grow short
when you reach September.

—Knickerbocker Holiday

OUR VOTES FOR QUOTES

Some guy described his Christian life by saying, "It's like grandmother's old bed: firm on both ends, but, boy! — it sags in the middle."

What you ARE speaks so loudly I can't HEAR what you say.

Sweet is the smile of HOME; the mutual look when hearts are of each other sure.

—*source unknown*

The important thing in life is not the triumph but the struggle. The essential thing is not to have conquered, but to have fought well.

—*Baron Pierre de Coubertin, founder of the modern Olympic Games*

Your WAS-ness doesn't matter, Your IS-ness is what am!

—*Ogden Nash*

EMILY: Do any human beings ever realize life while they live it, every, every minute?

STAGE MANAGER: No. *(Pause.)* The saints and poets, maybe — they do some.

—*lines from the play OUR TOWN, by Thornton Wilder*

FUN AND GAMES —
(For Grandparents & Grandkids)

SOLARGRAPHICS — (sun-sensitive paper — using pressed leaves or flowers under plexiglass or window pane glass)

CLAY — One of the most enjoyable diversions we've found is playing with clay. Even Granddads and teenagers enjoy making clay objects. I learned that F.A.O. Schwartz has the best clay; it will last years, and the clay productions are worthy of saving (I still have a couple of models that Lance and Scott made).

BUTTERFLY BOOKS

BIRD BOOKS

INSECT BOOKS

PARLOR GAMES: Scrabble, Yahtzee, Monopoly, Pictionary, Pictionary with Clay (F.A.O. Schwartz has this!), brain-teasers, Risk, Family Feud, Password, checkers, dominoes, magic tricks (there are many simple tricks in magic books), card games, Bunko, Bingo, jacks, riddles, (Kids know umpteen of 'em — and love to baffle the "experts". Buy a riddle book at a bookstore. You can ask riddles in letters and on the phone.)

MAKING DOLL FURNITURE (out of cardboard)

PAPER DOLLS

PING PONG

POOL

MAKING KITES...AND FLYING THEM

PRESSING FLOWERS AND LEAVES (It's easy to make presses.)

MARBLES

TOPS

ACTIVITIES

Recently I heard of a teacher who started children writing books in the first grade. As soon as they learn to write words, she encourages them to write stories about happenings real and imagined.

Children love to express themselves and can easily develop this skill. Encouragement is needed, of course — and praise! Show interest in their writing activity, and share yours as well.

Likewise, making up poetry and fun rhymes and sounds can become a game that will bring everyone fulfillment and create treasures.

LAST CHRISTMAS I was given an electric train — which is just what I had expressed a desire for. There was a method in my madness: I hoped the younger grandchildren would drop in often to play with it.

Last week Cooper came over and brought a worthy addition to the train's accessories: a whistle! The sound of it has enhanced the pleasure of enjoying the train.

I was quite touched by Cooper's present. "Gran'maw," he told me, "smell it — doesn't it smell good?"

It's a carved cedar whistle, one that Casey Jones would be proud of, and it *does* smell good. (I was gratified that this young boy appreciates and recognizes the good "smells" of wood!)

IN YOUR READING to grandchildren, start early reading poems and helping them memorize them. Memory work is a natural for them. Repetition is the key.

Repetition — doing or saying the same pleasant things again and again — has soothing and secure vibrations to everyone of all ages. Don't you feel comfortable with familiar places and faces? And we always value the repeated compliments and kindnesses that come our way. We hold them in our hearts to fall back on whenever we might feel threatened.

So in the best learning, repetition is a key. (Am I repeating myself?)

JOE AND DEBBIE JO'S CHILDREN began learning Bible verses early, and still continue that practice. Nightly the parents lie down at bedtime with each of their children, and as the day's doings wind down lightly and lovingly, Bible verses are repeated and recited, and new ones are learned. All the children can now recite entire chapters of the Bible.

In the same way, memorizing Scripture can be good for Gran'maw's mind. We grandparents can memorize along with the children. Such aerobic exercise of the gray matter racks up brain-power points, and I don't know about you, but I can use all I can get.

MAKING PANCAKES on Sunday evenings has been a many-times occasion with our family, and it's a fun supper to share with grandkids. Pancakes and pleasure are synonymous!

When I cook them, the house rule is "Don't wait for others to be served — eat 'em while they're hot!"

At the grill I make "dollar pancakes," pancakes in the shape of animals (everyone guesses what animal!), and short stacks. Finally, when everyone says, "Uncle!" I make the TEXAS pancake (all the batter that's left makes one BIG pancake!).

A variety of syrups—maple, blueberry, and honey-cream-and-butter—makes the eating an adventure.

Those special dishes for the family — the special foods only *you* can make — are an extremely important tradition to keep alive and well in the family, and for the grand-children to grow up knowing and tasting. (Our family always talks about "Gran'maw's rolls.")

I remember how my grandmother made cakes and fried pies all the time. How I loved to watch her beat the batter with her hand. And nothing could compare with the experience of "lickin' the batter"!

MEMORIES

**Do you ever think back on
the wonderful experiences you had
with your own grandparents
when you were a child?...**

I ASKED BOB, our eldest son, "What do you think of first when you think of Pardner?"

Without hesitation, he answered, "Fishing! She always took us fishing!" And she did. Pardner had a cottage on a private lake, and she went fishing every day of her life for years on end! She couldn't get enough of that "wonderful stuff."

Mother is a Hays, and the Hayses ALL loved to fish. I remember that when I was a girl, I sometimes went fishing with Mother and my Grandmother, but I nearly always took a book to read. My mother just swore I was left on her doorstep! No member of the Hays clan would rather read a book than fish!

I'm certain she thought I wasn't a "keeper," and would gladly have thrown me back in!

MY FRIEND Corrine, who works as a secretary at camp, remembers when it was time for each of the granddaughters (she was one of three) to go home after visiting their grandparents. Her grandfather would hold her little face between his big rough hands, and would lean down and whisper in her ear, "You are the BEST girl in the whole world!"

Corrine conveyed that for many years she believed that SHE — and only she! — was "the best girl in the world!" That impresses me as a magical way to make a child feel special.

MEMORIES

CORRINE also remembers seeing her grandparents stand outside on their porch as her family climbed into the car to drive back home. No matter how cold the weather, the grandparents would stand there, holding each other's hand and waving as Corrine's family drove away. The children watched until the grandparents — still waving — finally disappeared from sight.

Sound innocent and unimportant? No, indeed! That is MAJOR waving! Those grandchildren knew the grandparents loved them and hated to see them leave.

MY IRISH GRANDMOTHER on my mother's side was some special grandmother. Her shining hour was watching vaudeville shows, and when my brother and I were in her charge, we *loved* it!

We got on the streetcar in Dallas and went downtown, where three vaudeville theaters had regular shows. We attended all three the same day.

Another theater offered a burlesque show, and we were much older before we knew why Grandmother wouldn't take us to see that one. But we had had a long and full day. Our cup overflowed, and probably couldn't have held any more good stuff.

And then — was there anything to compare with the State Fair that Grandmother took us to every year? We would come home with a shopping bag brimming over with souvenirs from all the thrilling and exciting exhibits.

There are still many out-of-the-ordinary experiences to enjoy that will give your own grandchildren memories of us grandparents.

SCRAPBOOK

■ PART TWO ■

*Reflections
from our
Grandchildren*

COOPER

WHENEVER I COME up to your house you are very nice.

I like to play ping-pong with you, Pappy. You are so nice.

I like your peanut butter and jelly sandwiches, Gran'maw. You make good food.

They always take us on trips. They took us to Disneyland and Disney World and Epcot Center. They are always nice and considerate; they think of other people and they say nice things of other people. Once they start things they never stop. They always are nice to other people and thinking of everybody else.

• • •

BRADY

PAPPY'S best quality is being preservative — like when you were building at camp, you stuck to the work and didn't quit.

Gran'maw, your best quality is being hospitable. When people come into your house, you ask if they need anything.

My best times with you were:

Pappy, I remember you helping me build my first boat with.

Gran'maw, I remember the time you helped us build our little boats.

Pappy, I remember the time you helped us build the train Gran'maw got for Christmas.

Gran'maw, I remember when you and Pappy took us to St. Thomas, Hawaii, Disneyland, and Disney World.

I will teach my children to be preservant like you, Pappy, and to be hospitable like you, Gran'maw.

The thing that makes me want to go to your house is that you are giving, loving, and hospitable.

• • •

COURTNEY

YOU ARE ALWAYS such good examples for every one around you. You always serve everyone and are really Christlike. It just makes me want to grow up like you.

It makes me feel so good when you come to my soccer games and cheer for me. And Pappy, thank you for helping me make things and spending all your money on us. Thank you for being there when I needed you. I think it's really great when you can tell us something and Mom and Dad can't — it's like, we can take it better when you tell it to us, and it is really helpful to us and Mom and Dad. We can take it from you and it helps us a lot.

Pappy, you always come in the mornings to see how we are doing, and give us little game to play, and ask us how we are doing. You are really great about that.

When we walk through the woods together it's not just a walk through the woods. We stop and look at nature — how a leaf was formed, how a tree grows. We don't rush, we look. It helps us to forget about everything else and just enjoy nature. We look at what God has done for us.

You always make us feel like we are needed, like we are wanted. You always want us to come to your house to play a game of Yahtzee with you. You are always there and always have time for us. We know we can come up to your house any time we want and express our problems to you. I think that is really great. That's important.

You always make everyone feel welcome, even my friends. That's really great; it makes my friends and I feel really good.

Pappy is very unselfish, time-wise and material-wise. When the Super Bowl was on — and you know how no man would

miss it for anything — my friend Beth and I were at a health club and we didn't have anyone to come and get us. I called Pappy, and it was so easy for him: All he said was, "Oh yeah, I'll be there" — as if he wanted to do that more than anything in the world, including watching the Super Bowl. Then on top of that we forgot our money — ten dollars, as a matter of fact — and he was just as happy to give it as he was probably to get it.

Another of his qualities is perseverance. The way he built the bridge from one side of camp across the road to the other. He never quit.

Watching the way Gran'maw and Pappy care for each other is incredible. Gran'maw always makes him his special cereal, or packs his things when Pappy goes on trips.

I've just had a million great times with them...When they took Jamie and I to Alaska, they showed us every single place there was in Alaska. It just really meant a lot that you would want to spend your valuable time when you could be doing other things, but you decided to spend it on us.

Gran'maw always has time for me, or to do something for me. I wanted something cute to wear the last day of school and the last day of school was two days away. Yep, you guessed it — she had my dress done in one day.

She wants us to see the world with her. She and Pappy took us to Disney World, St. Thomas, Florida, etcetera. When we are sick or hurt, she always comes down to the house right when she hears about it. When I was sick she brought down markers and some paper; the rest of the day I had something to do instead of feeling sorry for myself.

• • •

JAMIE JO

YOU ARE REALLY THE COOLEST grandparents anyone could ever have, and I just thank you for being there for me through everything, all the difficulties and happiness in my life. You always listen with intent, and are excited about whatever I say. You are really picture-perfect grandparents.

When I'm stranded out in the middle of nowhere, you come pick me up. You laugh with us and play with the dogs.

You teach me so many things, like helping me with my homework. It's always good to have a smart Grandfather who can quiz you on math, and a creative Gran'maw and Grandfather who can help you with a science project.

You're someone I can talk out my problems with.

All the fun times — like when we had tea parties, or built snowmen, or played in the pond and cleaned it out, or made boats, or just ran and jumped in the leaves, or played with the dogs — you were always there, having fun. You act like you're thirteen years old, and it has really been fun growing up with you.

Your house has been like my second home, and when Mom and Dad are away you're my first home. In the morning I come up and eat breakfast with you at about five or six, and come sneak up on Pappy when he is doing his back exercises. That is really funny because I try really hard not to laugh, and you always try to get me back.

You are just the coolest, and I owe you so much, and thank you for always being there for me. You've been so special to me, and such a good example of how Christ is and how I should live my life, so I can grow up to be as neat as you.

JAMIE JO

Pappy I just want to have the discipline that you and Gran'maw have, and I just want to do whatever you do — except I might not go hang-gliding.

Gran'maw and Pappy are both very outstanding grand-parents. They have many Christlike qualities but they each have one main quality that makes me and God smile.

Pappy is a very "I'm Third" man — that means putting God first in your life, other people second, and yourself third.

I remember one time when he and Cooper (my little brother) were walking across a frozen pond and they fell in. Pappy didn't immediately swim to shore; he picked Cooper up and made sure he got to shore safely in Gran'maw's arms. Then Pappy made his way sliding on the slippery muddy bottom, all the way to shore. Then he went to get warm clothes for Cooper before getting them for himself.

Now Gran'maw is a very "I'm Third" person also, but in a dif-ferent way. Gran'maw will stop and drop anything she is doing to help me, play with me, or even transport me anytime. I remember one time when she was balancing the camp's checkbooks — and that is a hectic job — I got strep throat and my parents weren't home. So naturally I called Gran'maw. When I got to her house, she didn't get me settled and then go right back to work — no, she made sure I was comfortable and had everything I needed, and then she played games with me.

I've spent a lot of time with Gran'maw and Pappy over the years. Sometimes Dad tells me to "Come home and visit us sometimes."

All the times I've spent with Gran'maw and Pappy have been keepsake times. But a few special times do stick out in my

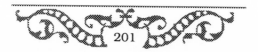

mind. Every spring we would clean out the pond behind their house. After the pond was cleaned we would turn on the waterfall to fill it up. While it was getting filled, Pappy would make all three of us boats, then we would race them down the stream and into the pond. Grandma would usually win.

I stayed with Gran'maw and Pappy a lot when I was little, because Mom and Dad were out of town. During the day, Gran'maw, Raggedy Ann, and Raggedy Andy and I would have tea and lemon drops at a tea party. We would also have M&M's. We would laugh for hours. I would always ask for just one more M&M, and Gran'maw would always give me one more. But she has a great picture of me pouting because she wouldn't give me another one.

Two years ago Gran'maw took me to Washington D.C. We had a blast. I loved seeing Gran'maw run around like a little kid. Boy did we put some mileage on our legs! We especially had fun trying to figure out the subways. If we got on the wrong one, we would get on the next one and go right back. Finally the last day we figured it out.

The things I look forward to when going to Gran'maw's house and Pappy's house are just spending quality time with them and learning from them so I can be just as good as they are and Christlike as they are when I get older. I just like talking with them or looking at slide shows from when we were little...and waking up in the morning and scaring Pappy when he's doing his exercises. Or just scaring Gran'maw anytime.

I know God is proud of them and I am proud of them.

• • •

WESLEY

MY GRANDPARENTS were good advisers. If I were any smarter earlier I would have realized that the advice they gave just about all the time turned out to be right. I didn't always follow that advice — sometimes I kinda wish I did.

I remember one time when I was with a bunch of my friends, and it was a Saturday afternoon and we were wanting to go shoot some pool, but we didn't have any money. So we all went over to my grandparents' house and went downstairs and shot pool, and talked to my Gran'maw and played games. We probably had a better time than if we would have gone to a pool hall.

My grandparents are just the type of people that if a stranger came up to the door and needed food, they'd feed him. And they're great friends. When you looked for someone to turn to, and you didn't really want to turn to your parents, my grandparents were always there.

This past year my grandfather showed a great deal of love when he drove two thousand miles just to give me a kayak, and to stay with me a day and a half. He just drove down here for that. On the way I'm sure he stopped and saw a couple of other people, but his one main purpose was to see me, and that makes you feel loved greatly.

I remember one time I was really upset at my Dad and I couldn't really go to him and talk about it — I didn't know how to do that (I wasn't too great at it at first). So I went to my grandparents and they were there and they told me what they thought, and helped me through it. They told me to give some slack, and — they were just there when you needed it.

You can pretty much sum it up in that one sentence: They were always there when you needed them.

WESLEY

All the trips they planned were great. I think sometimes I didn't appreciate my grandparents as much as I should have. In fact, I'm not too great at writing them; I know I could be better, but I don't do it too often.

Spike is what most people would probably call adventurous. I think he's done just about everything you can think of in sports. I remember when he told me he was going to kayak the ten toughest rivers in America. I saw those rivers. I didn't know what to think; I knew I wouldn't go down 'em. But he did and had a great time.

When I was up in Missouri last Christmas and saw the family, I wanted to see some friends too, and one of them didn't appear. So my grandparents offered me one of their new vehicles, brand new, to go find him. Boy, that just surprised me — I guess it shouldn't have, but it did.

I remember my grandparents as go-getters, and full of joy, loving everyone and everything. Darnell, my grandmother, reminds me of — kinda like an angel in disguise. She's always happy, never seems to be sick or anything.

My grandparents aren't the type to back down from any challenge. Both of them accepted challenges and trials of life in general. They'd go after 'em, they'd go get 'em. They aren't real laid-back, you know. They're strong and full of energy. They go and go until they accomplish whatever they're after.

I remember them staying by me after I was in a car wreck. They were always there encouraging me.

At Christmastime or whenever Scott and Lance and I were up in Missouri, we'd go to my grandparents' house and we'd all get up in the morning and head to the breakfast table,

and Gran'maw would be there waiting, and she'd say, "What do y'all want to eat?" And whatever we told her, she'd cook.

We all learned manners at home but it really went into practice at Spike and Darnell's house...which was fine with me, it's a great thing to learn.

She always made pecan pies, because all the White boys loved it. But you know, she kept diet Cokes, I remember, in one of the hallway closets just for me, since I'm a diabetic.

We did what they asked us to and stuff, but it just wasn't the same as at home. It seemed that you wanted to do more for them, because of what they did for you. It was just different. My grandparents made me feel that you would do anything they asked. A lot of times at my house I remember questioning my Dad: "Why do I have to do it?" I don't remember doing that at anytime at my grandparents' house. It was just a different sort of love. I remember feeling real warm and comfortable at their house — just a feeling, just their love and their warmth for you, and their wanting you to be there, and wanting to know what was going on. The excitement that they felt for you just made you feel great.

I remember many Christmases when all the grandkids would be around their house. It was funny because you'd see some presents under the tree, but she always kept ours hidden. It was kind of a game that we played every Christmas: We would try to find our presents, and I don't think any of us found them, ever. We never figured out where she put them.

A lot of times of course it was cold and there was snow on the ground, and Gran'maw would have hot oatmeal waiting when we got up, and she made sure we all dressed warmly,

and it was just that feeling of security you had at their house. It was just a great feeling. Kind of hard to explain.

At Easter we'd have Easter egg hunts all over what Spike called Whippoorwill Hill. Gran'maw was always planning stuff like that for you, fun things to do, that included not just you but the whole family.

Both my grandparents are real religious — which is good; I am too — but they were just always putting it in practice. Of course, it rubbed off on us.

Spike always gave the "I'm Third" talk at camp: God's first, others second, and I'm third. As I think about this, one reason he could give that talk so well is because he lived it, and so did Gran'maw. Like the saying goes, they practiced what they preached. And everything they preached was good: finding the good in others, helping other people out, stuff like that. They both loved to meet people, and they both went out of their way to help people.

It seemed like my Grandfather was always finding something new to do, and Gran'maw was always working and playing. They just had a good time.

I think they got us kids pretty much where we are today. They guided us and they got us to where we knew what was right and wrong.

The more I think about it, I try to put their practices to work. It's a great feeling when you do something like that. A lot of times when I had difficulties my grandparents were kinda like a big steamroller, smoothing things out and keeping them going.

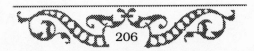

WESLEY

Spike and Darnell are a real loving couple. They love each and love the world. They always kept everything green and clean around camp. They love the birds and the animals, and they wouldn't harm anything in the world. They were loving folks. They loved everyone. And they were forgiving folks. If you messed up they would tell you what you did wrong, and they would forgive you.

I just wish I could see them more now that we're far apart. You really don't realize how much you miss folks like that until you get away from them, like I did. For a long time I guess I kind of took them for granted, but when I moved away and didn't get to see them so much I realized how much they meant and how much they taught me.

You just don't see folks like them around very much.

• • •

SCOTT

I CONSIDER Spike and Darnell's house in a way as more my home than my home here. It's filled with so many memories, and the memories are in the pictures there of so many things we have done, and the different objects in the house. It's so neat to look back at the pictures to see our whole family together: Spike, Darnell, her mother Pardner, and Mom and Dad and all our cousins and aunts and uncles, and going together on different trips. It's a neat environment to be in, a neat experience. Our whole family is represented there.

Spike and Darnell — Gran'maw and Pappy — were on all those trips and were probably — definitely — the center of all those trips, giving us all the entertainment and just being as fun or funner than anyone else, and being right there. And it's not that I love them just because they sent us on these trips, but they were right there with our family, having fun and giving us fun.

Spike took my brother Lance and my cousin Wesley and me one summer to a place called Nantahala Outdoor Center to learn to kayak; the three of us boys had never kayaked before. That was probably the most memorable and funnest trip of my life. Spike didn't spend all the time with us; he let us learn. He didn't stand by and hold our hand and say, "You need to do this with the kayak, and this." He sort of explained it on the way up there, and when we got there he let us off and he went and did his own thing. We saw him a lot during the day and he didn't leave us — we always felt secure and knew he was still there — but we would be floating down the river and we would see him taking pictures or floating by us in his kayak. He was always there, but he let us learn. And always, throughout my life I remember Spike putting me in instances where I had to do something on my own; he wouldn't hold my hand. I had to

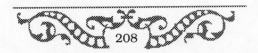

do something on my own and learn it. At the time it was kind of uncomfortable for me, because I wished he had done it· for me. But I look back and I notice that I've learned as much from Spike as from anyone. He's just an incredible man.

Darnell is very funny, very lively, just a neat person to be around. She's very supportive of everything Spike does, and I think that's very important. And she is also very supportive of whatever we do. If it's a good decision, and hopefully it is, she is behind you one hundred percent. She encourages you.

They are very patient all the time. If we do something wrong they don't jump on our backs, but they let us try and figure it out. I think that is something that has helped us learn.

I try to spend as much time with him as I can. I consider him my best friend. It's so neat to hear him talk, and to listen to him, cause he's been through so much, and he is so knowledgeable that you can learn a lot from him.

A grandkid has to be able to want to learn, and I haven't always been. A long time ago I remember trying not to listen to Pappy because he did talk a lot and he did know a lot, but I just didn't care about learning. But there comes a point in your life where you just want to know a whole lot more. And Spike's the person to learn a lot from.

Last summer Spike and I went back to Nantahala Outdoor Center and I took some more kayaking courses, and he went kayaking on some other rivers. I tried not to sleep on the trip up there because it's quite a ways to North Carolina, and I just tried to listen to him and get him to talk about his experiences and what he thinks about this and that. I think it's

SCOTT

very important to listen to him and get to know what he's known and...well, I've gotten to know him a whole lot more the more time I spend with him and let him talk about his experiences or his knowledge or what he thinks as far as the Bible goes, or friendship, working, hobbies and stuff.

Gran'maw and Pappy are both characters. They are unique. They aren't like any other; they are their own personality, and they don't change it for us. And they show all their character — they show their bad side and good side. They don't hide their feelings when they think something is wrong. They will tell you how they feel, and sometimes very strongly. At times you just don't like them telling you that strongly, but you look back on it after a while and figure it's probably a good deal, and you learn a lot from it.

My cousin got in trouble with the law this summer and Spike and Darnell let him know that he'd done wrong. He knew he had, and he felt very badly about it, but they didn't just let it stop at that; they let him know, and they were very strict on him. But they were very patient in the situation, and they forgave him. Everything's fine now.

I think grandparents should take a stand as far as what they think, because I have noticed a lot of my friends' grandparents really don't take a stand; they just kind of don't say anything. They just don't want to displease their grandchild that they love so dearly. They don't want to get on their bad side, and so they don't say anything. I think they should, though not so ferociously that it makes everything real bad. It's just not good then; the child won't want to be with the grandparent and all of that. But to the point that everyone can learn from the situation, they should say what they think.

SCOTT

Spike and Darnell are very talkative. They tell us about different experiences, which is really fun — we just kind of sit around and talk, and I like to do that. It's neat to be with them.

They take us a lot on trips, and give us a lot, but they don't shower us with gifts every time we see them. They give us experiences, neat experiences. I think that's a lot more important — experiences we can talk about with our own grandchildren, about our grandparents. Other grandparents I know of give their grandchildren all kinds of stuff, and then that's all the grandchild expects from the grandparent — just gifts. I think you should give them *time,* and that's what Spike and Darnell give to us a lot — well, not as much as I would like, but as much as they can spare. It is kind of hard though; they're up in Missouri and we don't get to see them a whole lot, but when we do I cherish the moment.

It has been neat being able to spend the time with them going on trips, seeing different sights with them, and to look at Spike and Darnell, and to know they're looking at something and they're saying, "That's really neat," rather than sitting back and thinking, "I already know this; I'm older and I've been around, and I know all of this." They're just as young as we are on those trips, and just as active. And they're trying to learn just as much as we are.

• • •

LANCE

DARNELL WRITES REALLY FUN letters, and she writes pretty often. And though they're a long way away — they live in Missouri and we live in Texas — I feel as if we are there because she tells funny stories, and she describes what's been going on in her life and Spike's. She also puts jokes in her letters. They may be corny jokes, but they're really hilarious, especially the fact that they're coming from a grandparent.

Spike and Darnell go out and do stuff with us. They make things happen. (Remember that: *They make things happen.*)

Once I was going bow-hunting, and was going to be up in a tree. I asked Spike if he wanted to go, and sure enough he went with me. So here we were up in the same tree. He tied himself in, and ended up falling asleep up there. I didn't get anything, but it was still fun just to look up there and see Spike asleep, all tied in just to keep himself from falling out of the tree — and just the fact that he spent time with me, he went out there in the woods to bow-hunt with me.

One time — and there are many examples like this, but this is just one — I wasn't too excited about going on a canoe trip but Spike really wanted us to do this, he wanted us to go and float down the Navasota River. It ended up that I was so glad I went, because he made it fun.

About seven years ago Spike, Scott and I had set traps for coons, and here was ol' Gran'maw going out with Scott and me to check the traps. Sure enough we got about three or four coons, and if you know coons, you know they get kinda heavy, especially when I was only about twelve years old and Scott was eleven. So Gran'maw carried them the whole way back to the car, which was about a mile or a mile and a half, and that's a heavy load. Just think, she went out there with

LANCE

us and did that for us. That's just cool. Not many grandparents would go out in the woods with you, much less
carry your coons for you.

They also get the whole family to go on trips with them,
which is kind of a tradition on Thanksgiving. We are fortunate to be able to do that. When we go on trips they also
want us get something out of it — not just to go and have a
blast, but that we would also gain something. For example,
when we went to Washington D.C., and Williamsburg,
Virginia, we went and we read all the stuff. I really appreciate that now; back then I don't think I appreciated it as
much.

We went to the British Virgin Islands and went sailing and
that was a blast, on a big ol' fifty-foot boat. Spike brought
along scuba tanks and I wasn't very excited about going
scuba diving, but sure enough he got us going, and I did it
and I had a blast. I loved it. He made things happen.

Spike and Darnell love us, and they are there to watch us,
but even more they participate in the things we do. They're
active in our lives, they're not just passive about things; they
want to get involved too.

I'm really proud of them. I like to brag about my grandparents. It makes it so much easier to love your grandparents if you're proud of them and like to brag on 'em...I'm
real fortunate because not very many old people are able to
do as many things as Spike and Darnell — such as Spike
still building camps, and Gran'maw still working there; and
Gran'maw "woggs" — she walks and jogs in intervals, and
she calls it "wogging." Spike goes hang-gliding and
kayaking. And they both speak on occasion at camp and
such. They have great deal of respect amongst others.

They are also really proud of us, and they tell us that they are proud of us and of the things that we do, and they point out our good qualities.

Something else I think is neat is that they know when to tell us that we've messed up. But they don't overdo it by getting overly involved with our lives to the extent that they get into things they don't exactly know about, when our parents might know us better in that certain area.

Their enthusiasm is contagious. We may live a long ways away from them — I see them about twice a year — but when we are with them it is quality time. Oh, it's fun to be with them.

They didn't overflow me with riches like material goods — going out and buying stuff at stores — but instead spent *time.* That's the thing I remember.

When I was younger, about six years old, I was big-time into Indians. I loved Indians. And Darnell actually researched how to make me an Indian outfit — she made drums and moccasins and a headdress; she made every thing Indians had. She researched it to find out exactly how to do it just right, and that's exactly what she did. Making that outfit for me that was just cool. One time she also made me a karate uniform that I just loved; I wore it around everywhere for a while. I love them to death; they are so freakin' easy to love.

There is one more thing I would like to point out that is very obvious; and that is, that they are so Christlike. Something that comes to mind when I say that, is that a number of times I have seen my Grandfather get down on his knees before he goes to bed, and pray for ten minutes. This is a man seventy-five years old, getting down on his knees and

LANCE

praying to God before he goes to sleep. That's just incredible. And I remember one time, when he was preparing for a speech, he bowed down and prayed to God for help. And when he prays, he doesn't just do that right in front of me; it just so happened that I was in the room. In fact, one time I wasn't in the room — I just peeked in for a second. But they're really Christlike, and they continually apply Christ to their life.

• • •

CODY

WHEN MOST PEOPLE think of grandparents, they think about a couple of people sitting on the front porch waiting for the grandkids to come home, or talking on the telephone to all their other friends, or watching TV. But that's just not the way my grandparents are.

Gran'maw and Pappy are just incredibly great. They have taught me a lot about life, helped me grow up, helped make me the person I am, which hopefully is pretty good. They taught me just a lot about life as far as working goes.

They're not perfect, but they're as perfect as you can get on earth probably.

Gran'maw is probably the best influence I had in my childhood. My brother has diabetes and epilepsy, and he was a little kid when he was diagnosed. They thought he was going to die. He was up in St. Louis at a children's hospital, and when my Mom and Daddy were with him, my Gran'maw took care of me. That's the reason we were so close, because we spent a whole lot of time together, and to me Gran'maw was number one.

She would take me fishing. There aren't too many Gran'maws who will go fishing with you and bait your hook. We did it all the time, any time I wanted to. We caught a lot of big ones, I promise you. Gran'maw could fish with the best of them.

When I was a little kid going to camp, Gran'maw would always come down to see me. That meant a lot, especially as homesick as I was.

Probably the most important thing Gran'maw taught me was to appreciate reading — that's as good as you can do for

anybody, I think, nowadays. She had a big library down-stairs, and she would spend hours reading to me down there, and when I learned how to read I would read to her. I'm sure she got bored listening to me fumble through the English vocabulary. I developed a great love for reading, and I still have that today.

Gran'maw taught me about manners — over and over again, believe me! My Mom and Dad taught me a lot about manners, but nothing like Gran'maw. She was the one who drove the point home. You didn't go over to her house and put your fork in the wrong place, or chew with your mouth open, or not hold a lady's chair for her or hold the door open for her, and everything like that. And if I said something like, "There ain't nothing going on," then I would have to repeat "There is not anything going on" ten times; that's the way she would drill it into my head.

My Gran'maw isn't the best athlete in the world — she is a lot more petite and lady-like than she is athletic. But she would go down there in the basement with me and play pool at the pool table — I'm sure it wasn't her favorite sport, but she knew how to have a good time anyway. And she would shoot baskets with me at camp. She would do anything I wanted. She would go out of her way to help you.

When I was in junior high — and you know how, when you're a kid, you worry about how you dress and everything — I began to notice that my Gran'maw was always in style; she always looked hip. Whatever the kids in school had on, Gran'maw had on — and she probably wore it first.

And another thing: Gran'maw has a great sense of humor — it's probably where my Daddy got it from. She's just real witty. She always comes up with funny things to say.

CODY

When I got into junior high I got into sports, probably my favorite thing to do. I got into boxing and that was probably not a Gran'maw sport — she didn't like it a whole lot, watching me bleed, and get my face punched in. But she would always be there at the matches, taking pictures (all the pictures I have, she took), and I know she didn't like it at all. She sure was glad to see me quit that.

When I got into high school I started to date. Gran'maw always got along with my girlfriends; she always loved them. She would invite them over and eat with them and talk for hours, and talk with them on the phone. In fact, my girl-friends probably cared more for her than they did for me. She was great about that. Everybody loved Gran'maw.

One of her favorite things is a little ol' Spitfire, a British car, and once in my senior year I wanted to borrow it to take a girl out (I drove an old truck). Gran'maw gave me the keys and I took off. On the way back home I wasn't paying atten-tion, and I ran right into the back of a guy. It didn't really damage his car, and he was a good guy and let me go and didn't say anything, because all I did was hurt Gran'maw's car. I went over to Gran'maw's house and knocked on the door, and I mean I was scared — I felt so bad because I wrecked the car. She came out there and did the coolest thing: She just laughed! I could not believe it. She knew I felt bad and that I probably wouldn't do it again.

That brings up the point that Gran'maw is always cheerful, always smiling about something. She's an inspiration because she's always happy. I know she gets that through her Christian faith, and that should be an example for us all. You'll never go to Gran'maw's house and have her yell at you.

CODY

She's a true lady. I mean that in every sense — the way she dresses, the way she talks. You'll never hear her say a dirty word or use bad manners.

Another thing about Gran'maw is that she writes poetry; she writes it very well. She's very smart, and has a good mind.

I've messed up a lot of times, and Gran'maw has never let down on me; she was disappointed maybe, but she always comes back and smiles at me, and tells me she loves me, and gives me a hug...and that's the greatest. It makes me feel so much more confident in myself. I know she's proud of who I am and who I'm going to be, and she has a lot to do with that. She's still supportive of me in college and sends me "flags" (as the White family calls money), and that always helps out.

Even though I'm not the best at letter-writing, she is, and she always will be a great person.

Spike is somebody great to talk about. Spike is — well, he'll never quit; he just keeps on going.

When I was a little kid he used to take us hunting all the time in South Texas, and Pappy would always outdo us; he was out jumping around, ready to go. I remember when I was a little kid he would take us canoeing on the river. Not many granddads would get in a canoe with you, getting all wet and cold, running into rocks and snakes — but he'd do it all with you.

Whenever we would take trips as a family Pappy would always be the guide, the culture guide. He would have us stop to see every little thing there was to see. Pappy does it all.

CODY

The thing about Pappy, he's not one of those speakers who tells you something and does another thing. Pappy does it. He's not a hypocrite, neither he nor Gran'maw.

The greatest thing Pappy does is discipline. I remember when I got in my "talking back" stage at twelve or thirteen; if I'd talk back to my Dad, I'd probably keep talking back till I got a whipping. But with Pappy, if I talked back to him when he was telling me something, he would just give me "the look," which was a kind of squint. I'm telling you, it would rock you right back in your shoes. Believe me, I never talked back after he gave me that.

When Pappy got mad at you or was disappointed in you, he never yelled at you; he would give you a little talking to. After you got done talking to him, he'd just forget about it and that was it. You didn't hear about it again.

When I was a kid, my Daddy and I had a ranch, and Pappy would always come out and help. He would be out there in the cold weather digging fence-posts, building barns — he would do it all, I tell you.

Pappy and Gran'maw are blessed financially, but he is a common folk. That's something I love. I promise you that he would treat some wino carpenter who came into his house just as good as he would the President. Everybody is treated the same — great. Gran'maw too for that matter; they're both that way. He is a common folks man.

Pappy's hilarious. He rides around with an ol' dog in his truck, the hair all over it and it stinks and stuff...I always remember Gran'maw telling me about the man who said, "Spike is the commonest rich man I ever met." And that's what Spike is.

CODY

Pappy just keeps on refusing to grow old.

He makes friends everywhere; everyone is his friend.

Just from being around Pappy in my younger days, he has taught me the work ethic, how to work hard. And he's an example. He and his crew that helps him build the camps, not a one of them is under sixty years old. I worked construction three summers, and they work harder than anyone I've ever seen, and just as fast. They're incredible.

Pappy and Darnell — together they've gone through their whole lives with nothing but a smile. They're thrilled, and everything's been fun. They've filled everything up. They've worked hard together, and they continue to work hard and help other people. They've become living legends.

Something that happened recently that really opened my eyes about them, is that my Mom and Daddy were separated when I was a senior, and ended up getting divorced. Through it all Pappy and Gran'maw never failed to keep in touch with my mom, and make her still feel like part of the family. Spike goes to see her, and she's always grateful to them for that. When she got married to Ray, and moved to West Texas, Spike went out there and met him.

And they helped my Dad through everything. He got married to Delisa, and she's a great person herself. And they accepted her as part of the family, just as they had everyone else. They were great about that. They didn't hold any grudges and they didn't show any signs of taking sides. They just loved them through the hurt.

They continue to support the family and to help me through school. And they continue to write me (and that's one thing I

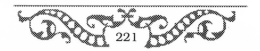

want to get better at, is writing). Gran'maw has her new computer and she spits those letters out like nobody's business. I get at least one or two letters a week from them.

Spike and Darnell are totally happy together. I'm sure they fight sometimes, because everyone has their differences — but they'll never do it in front of you. They'll just drop it, they give ground; each of them gives ground, because each one is different. They just have a great loving relationship. They love each other a ton. They're *happy* — that's the word to sum it up, and that's how I want to be in life.

• • •